A GUIDE TO DRAWING BEAUTIFUL PLANTS IN NATURE

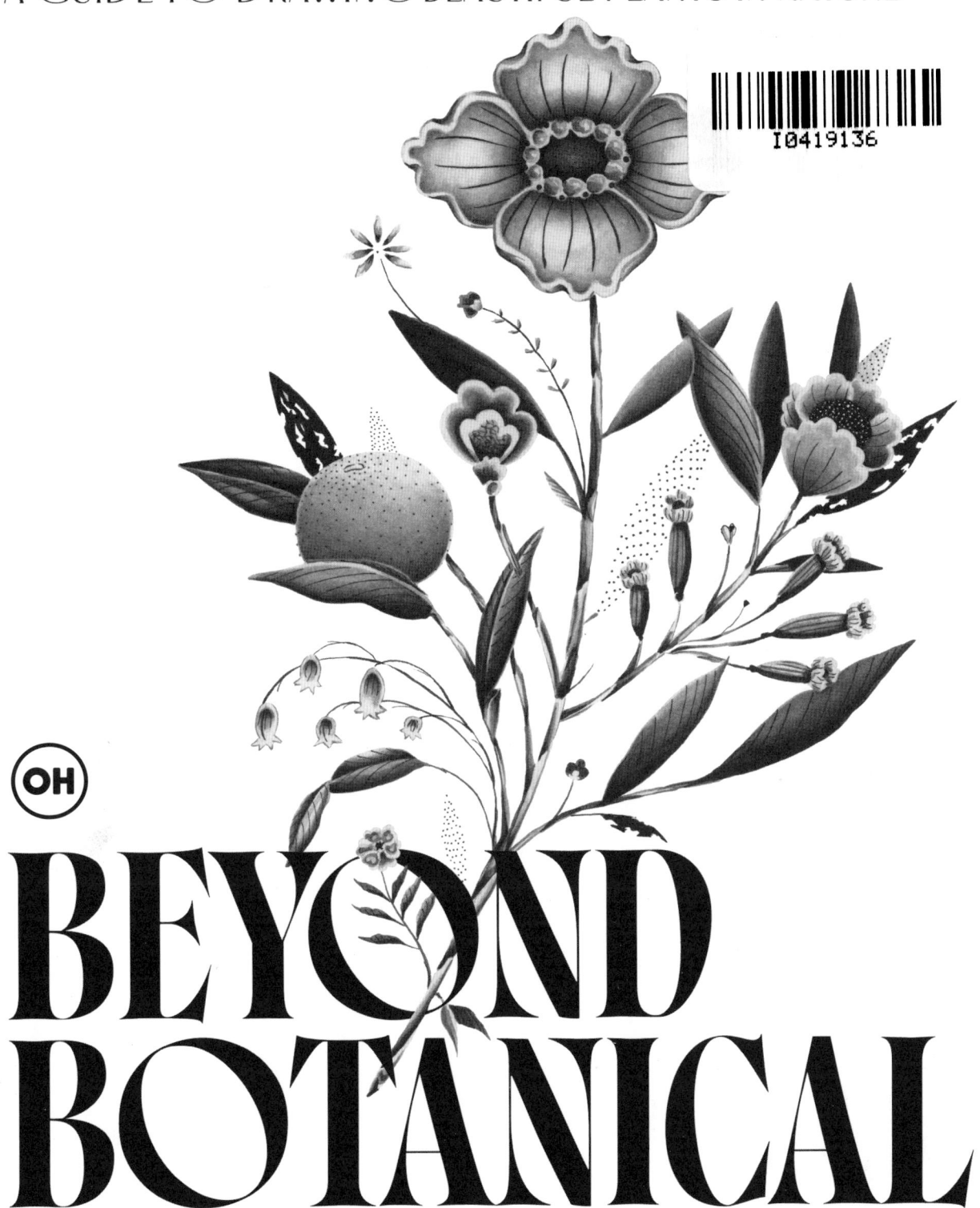

OH

BEYOND BOTANICAL

DANIEL THE GARDENER
Free-hand Botanical
Tattoo Artist and Painter

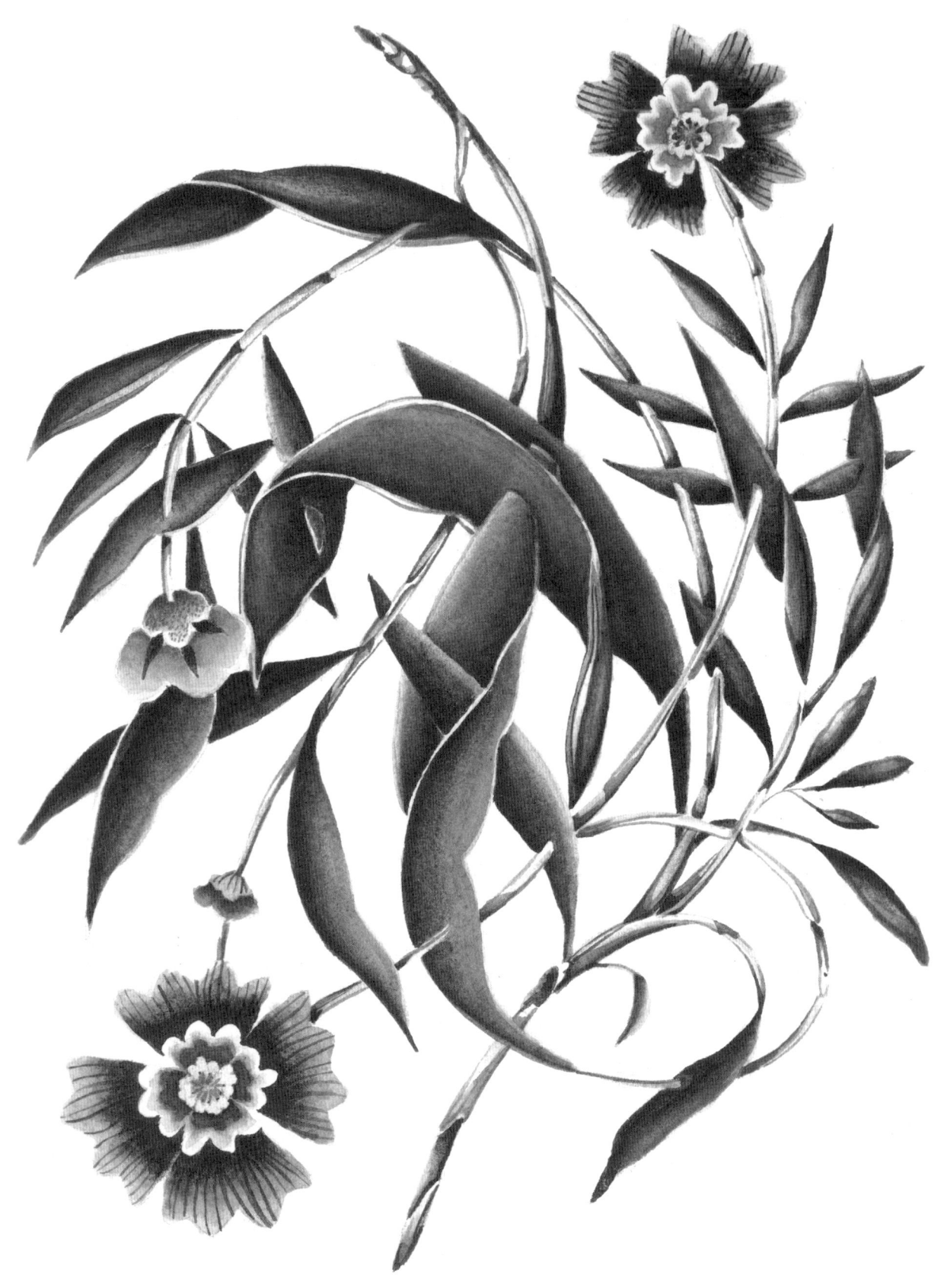

To Chris, who sang to earth, air, fire and water.

To Hermanosis, who guide me where plants keep their wisdom.

To Charlie, who brightens my heart every day of my life.

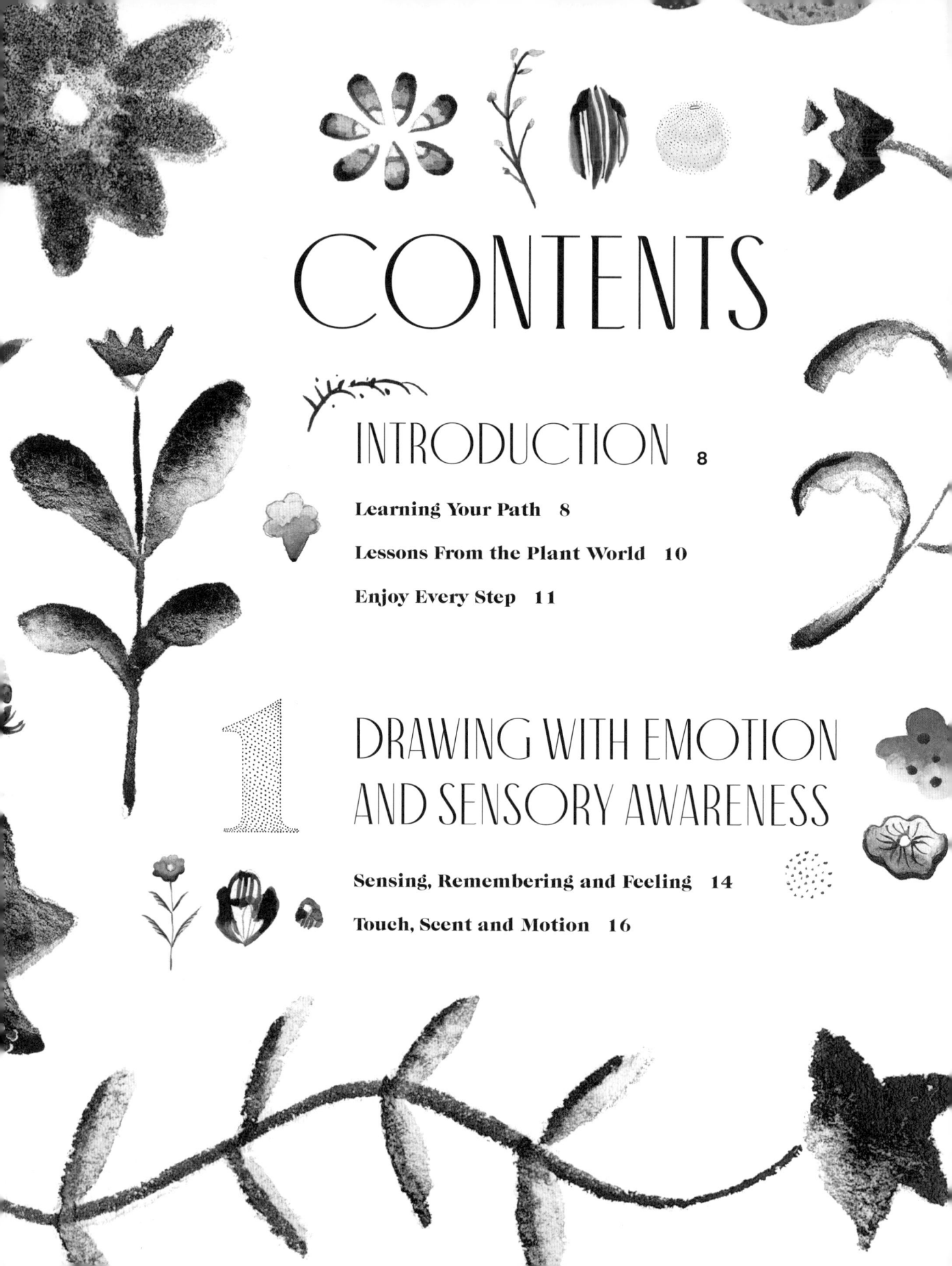

CONTENTS

2 FINDING YOUR WAY THROUGH TOOLS, TECHNIQUES AND SELF-EXPRESSION

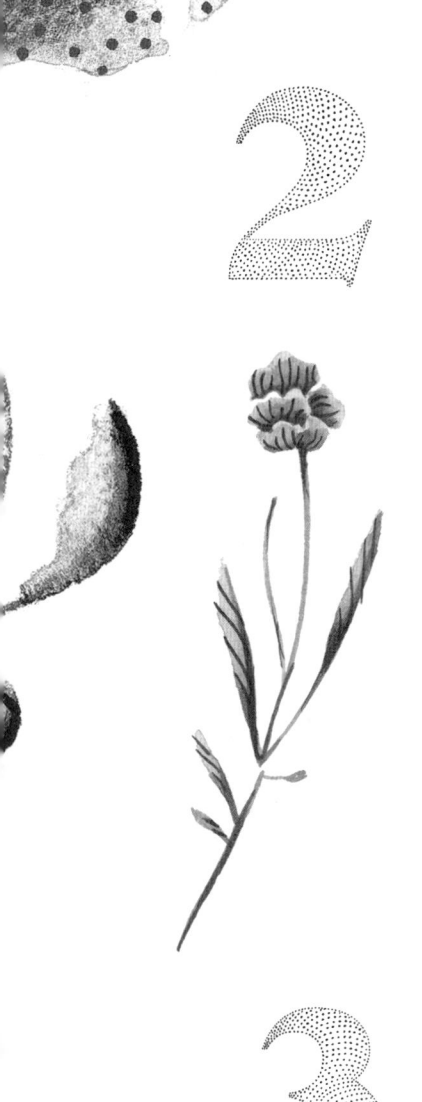
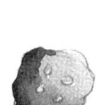
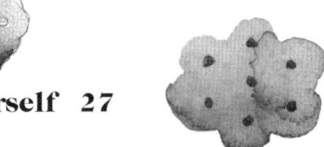

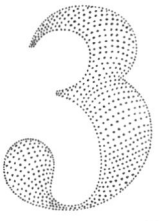
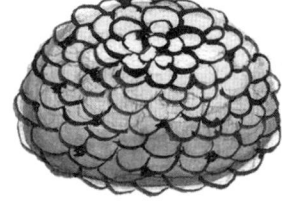

3 PLANTS AND WHERE TO FIND THEM

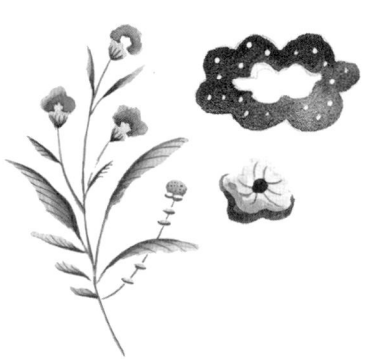
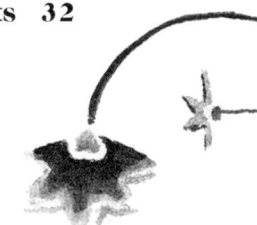

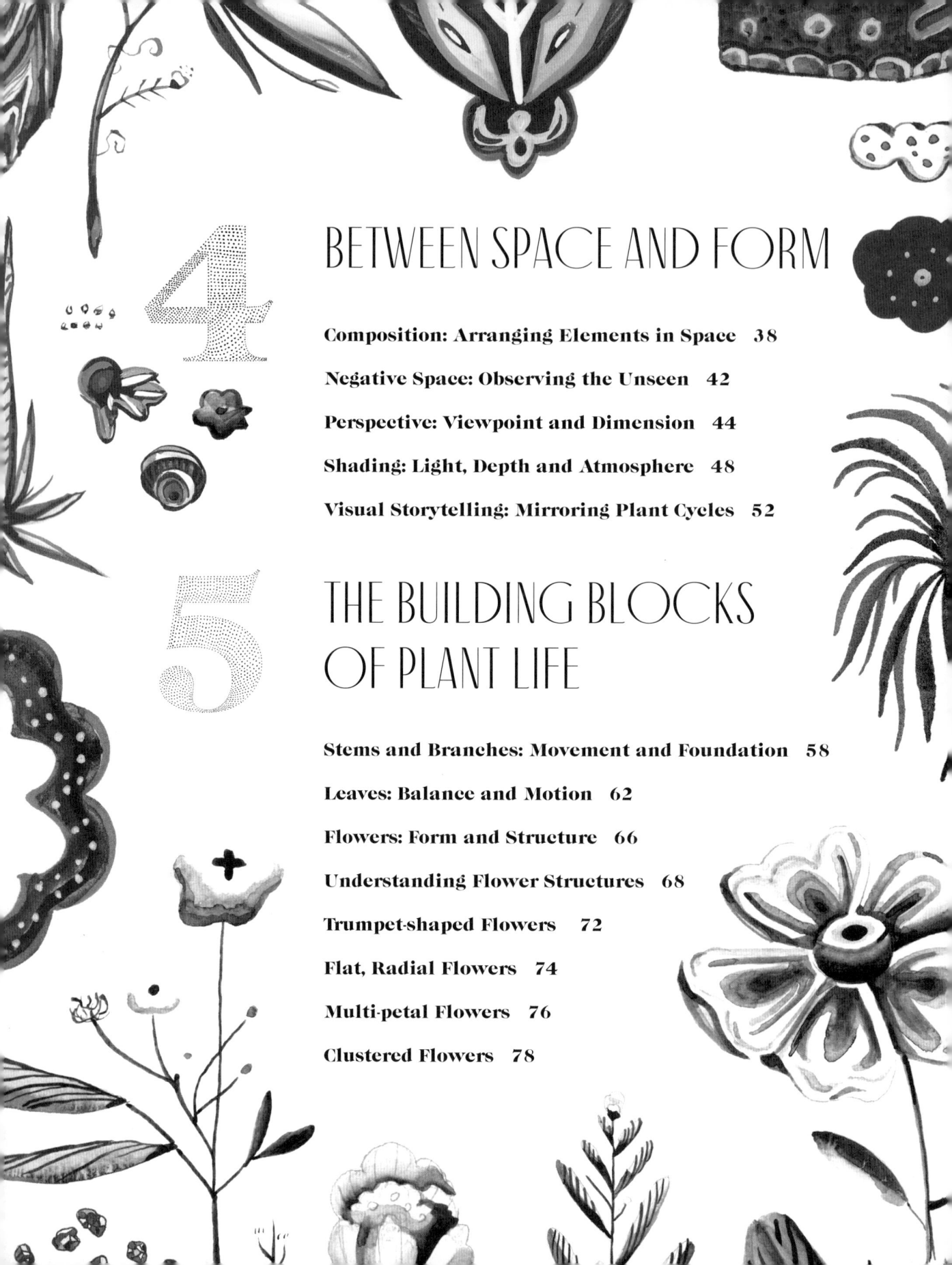

4 BETWEEN SPACE AND FORM

5 THE BUILDING BLOCKS OF PLANT LIFE

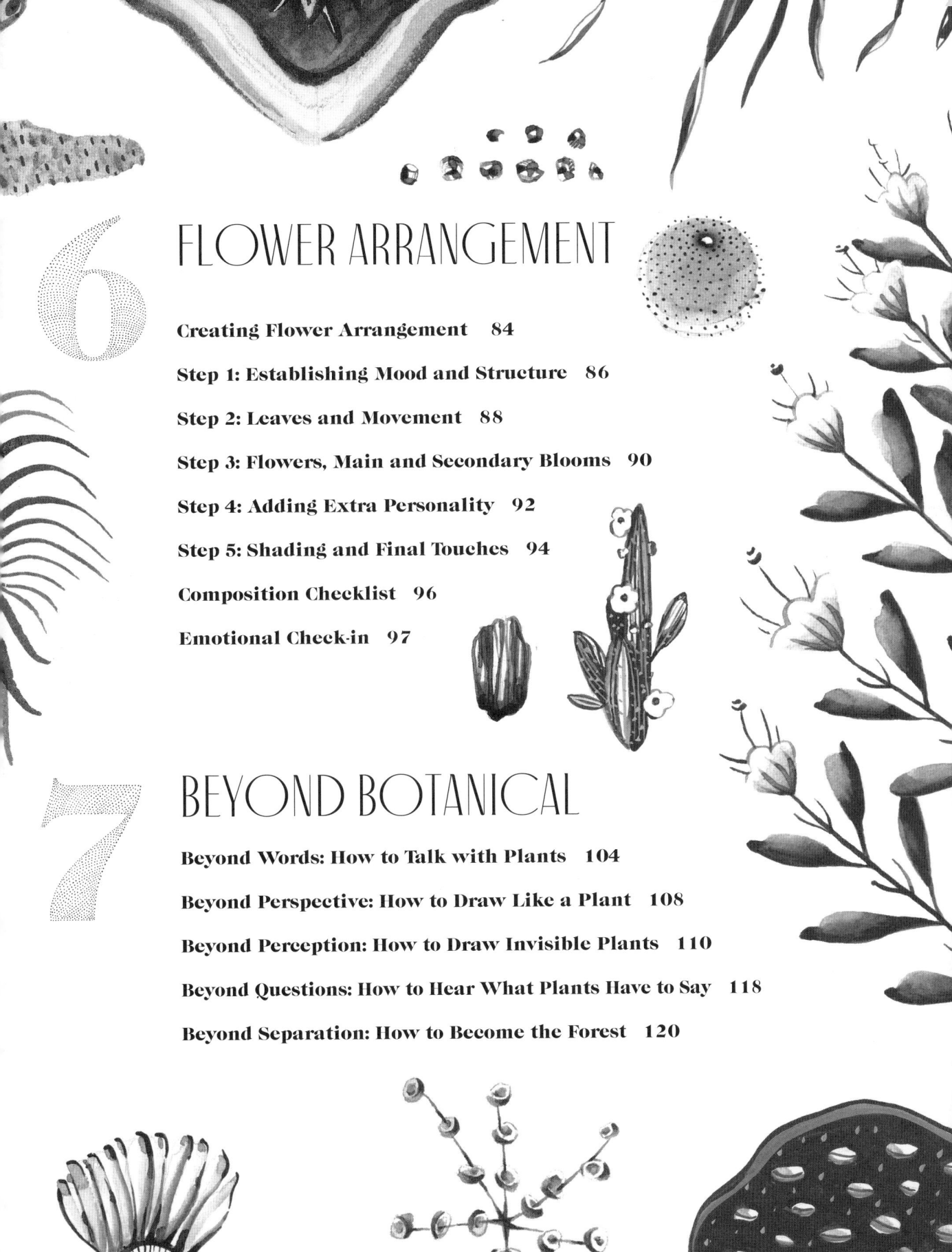

6 FLOWER ARRANGEMENT

7 BEYOND BOTANICAL

INTRODUCTION

LEARNING YOUR PATH

This book is for anyone who wants to draw plants. More than that, it will help you to illustrate in a way that also mirrors your emotions and your experiences with the flora around you.

We'll explore the fundamental elements of plant representation – those that make plants look like plants – and how to create well-balanced, complex arrangements. Throughout these pages you'll also find exercises designed to challenge your perception and image-making abilities. Some will take you for a walk in the park or to your local botanic garden, while others are best enjoyed from the comfort of your sofa with a cup of tea in hand.

Think of it less as a manual and more as an exploration of yourself, your creativity, the places you visit and the environments you inhabit. There's nothing here to achieve beyond deepening your sensitivity and love for nature. While a specific order is proposed to guide you along, this journey is yours to shape.

So, feel free to flick through the contents, skip around, revisit sections and approach each activity as many times as you like. Some exercises might resonate with you now, while others may become more relevant over time. Set your own pace – there's no rush, no fixed destination.

Let's begin.

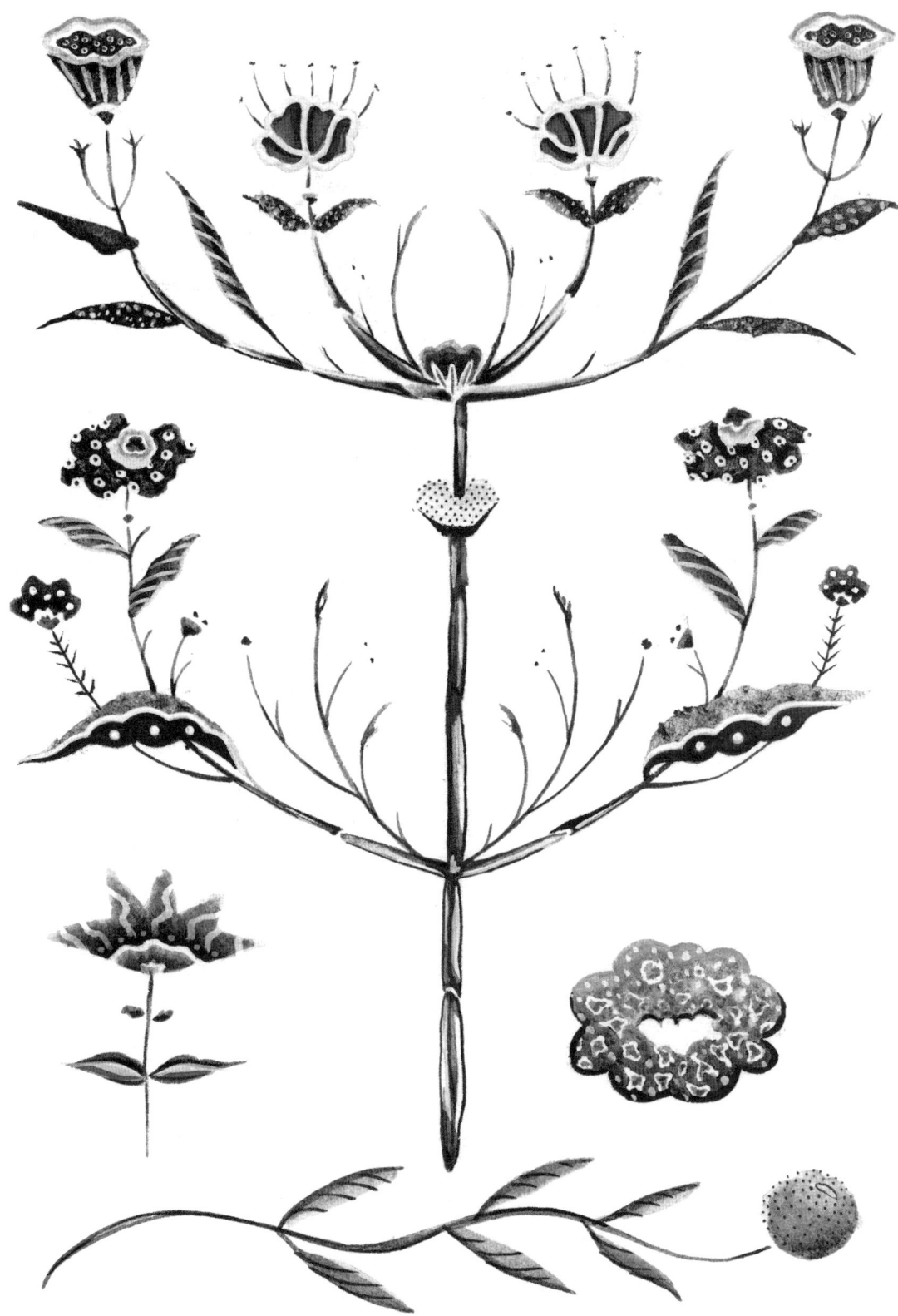

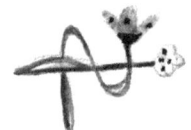 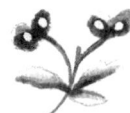 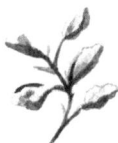 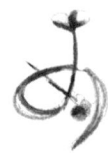 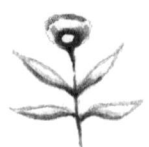

LESSONS FROM THE PLANT WORLD

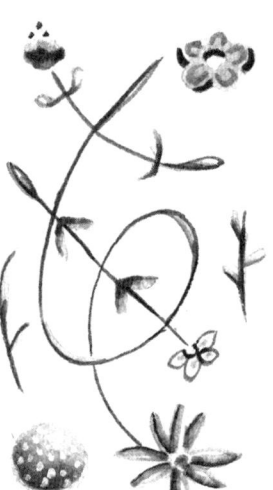

Plants are the foundation of life on Earth. They transform light and water into food and oxygen, capable of sustaining entire ecosystems.

They provide shelter, nourishment and protection for countless species, nurturing animals and shaping the landscapes we inhabit. Without them, life as we know it wouldn't exist.

With their powerful silence, they teach us lessons about adaptability, interconnection and subtlety. Thriving in the world around us, they move through cycles of growth, rest and renewal.

The practice of drawing plants can help us reconnect both with nature and ourselves, inviting us to a place where organic forms and shapes blend with one another, encouraging us to slow down and look inward. Through every gesture on the page, their forms become more familiar – and in that familiarity, we find a sense of inherent belonging.

Approach every plant as one living being encountering another; soften your presence, be humble and let openness guide you. Step beyond observation. Plants can reveal themselves in the most unexpected ways.

WHAT PLACE DO PLANTS HOLD IN YOUR LIFE?

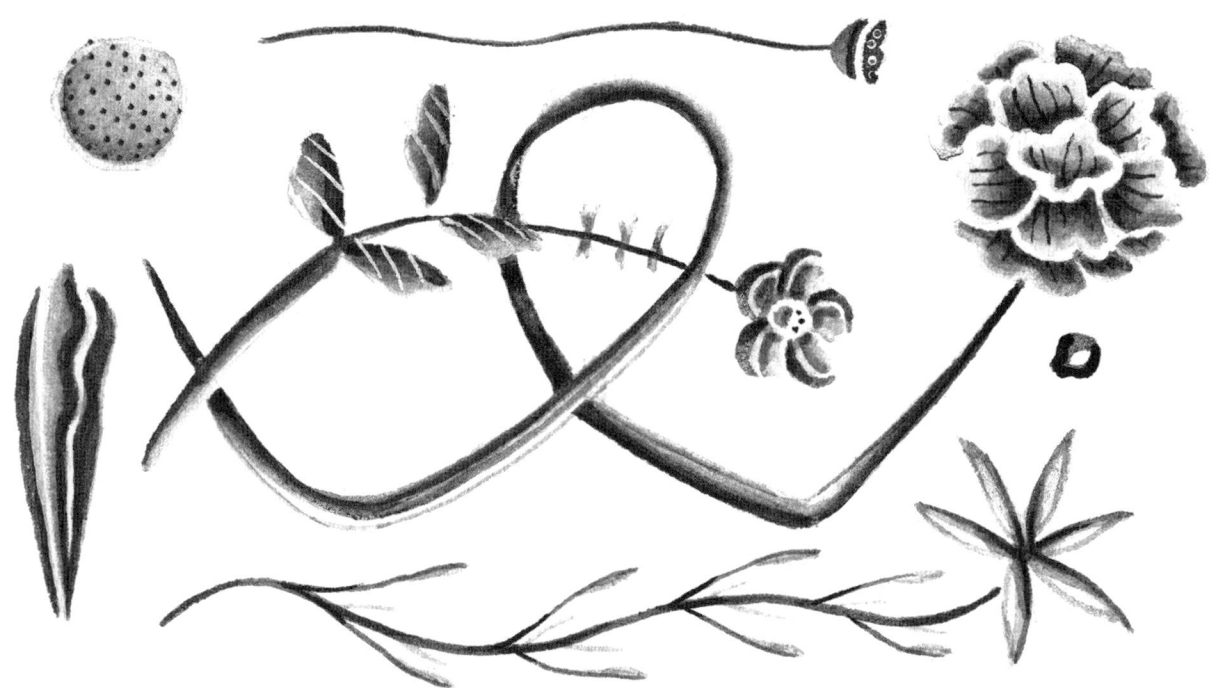

ENJOY EVERY STEP

There's a distinct feeling that comes with creating, and we are all drawn to the sense of fulfilment it holds. Learning to draw plants requires patience - not just with the practice but with yourself. It takes time for your skills to develop.

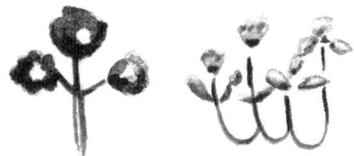

Remember that inspiration comes and goes. What matters most is coming back to your sketchbook, allowing the process to keep unfolding. Over time, the act of drawing becomes a space you can step into, where your imagination can express itself, free from the forces that govern our daily lives.

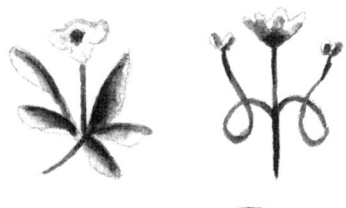

Your first steps are special. No matter how skilled you become, you will never return to this moment again. Slow down, enjoy every step and don't be afraid to stumble along the way.

Not everything you create needs to be shared; there's a quiet freedom in drawing without the weight of external validation. When you do invite feedback, be mindful of whose voices you let in. Take what helps, leave the rest, and remember: this is about expressing yourself in your own way, shaped by how you perceive the world around you.

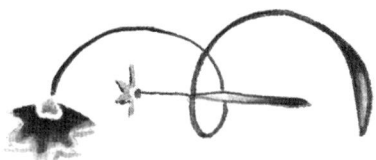

Drawing plants gently weaves us back into nature. Trust the process, and watch the universe unfold before your eyes.

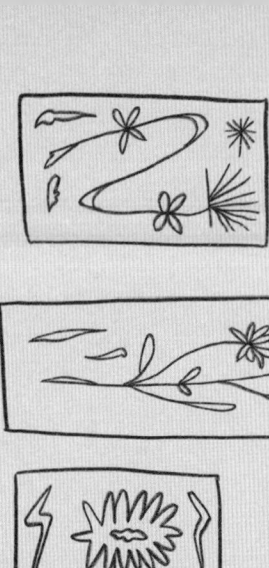
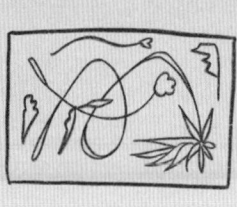
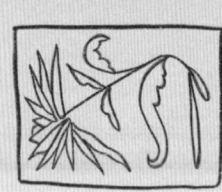
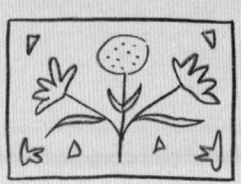

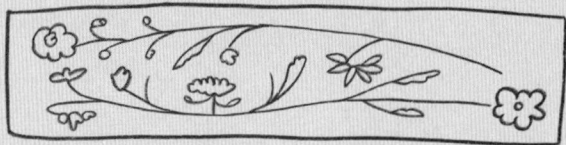
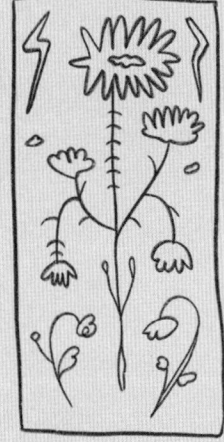
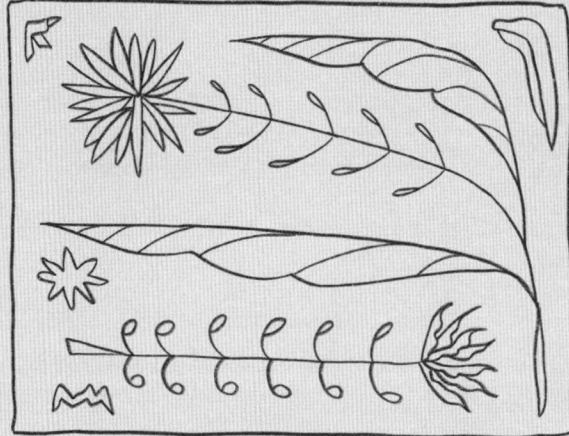
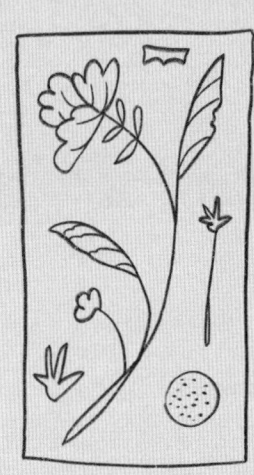

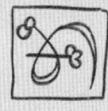
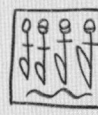
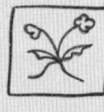

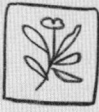

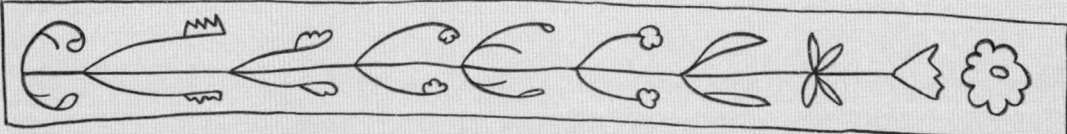

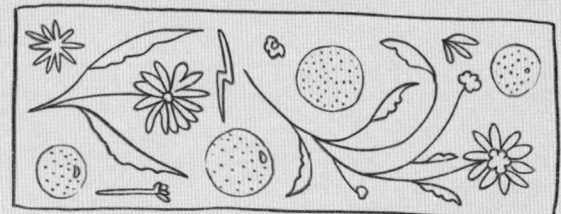

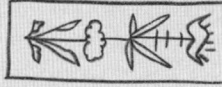
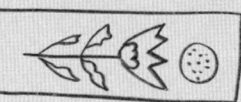

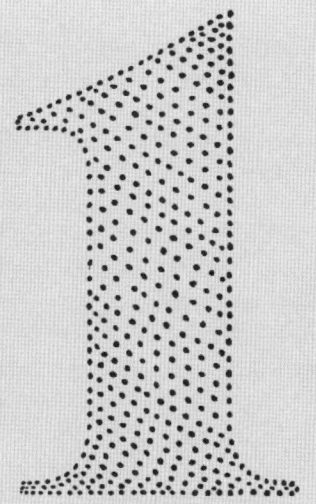

DRAWING WITH EMOTION AND SENSORY AWARENESS

Every drawing has an intention, and the way you understand and represent plants goes far beyond what your eyes alone can notice.

In this chapter, we'll uncover the ways your whole self recalls encounters with plants and explore how to let these impressions enter your illustrations, bringing forward what often goes unnoticed.

SENSING, REMEMBERING AND FEELING

Our perception of the world around us is shaped by more than just what we observe. While vision plays a dominant role, invisible forces, such as sensations, memories and feelings, also influence how we understand and interpret what's around us.

These forces leave traces on us – whether we're fully aware of them or not – and they naturally find their way into our creative work. A plant that reminds you of your childhood garden, a parent's favourite flower or a meaningful place you once visited may stir something within you that subtly influences your marks.

Maybe you instinctively soften the lines, exaggerate a particular movement or choose colours that evoke a certain mood. Even when we think we're simply 'drawing what we see', we are always making choices about what we emphasize and what we leave behind, guided by previous experiences in our lives.

By allowing yourself to engage with plants beyond just their physical form, your illustrations will begin to reflect the myriad other influences that inform your perception.

WHAT ARE YOUR MOST MEANINGFUL MEMORIES WITH PLANTS?

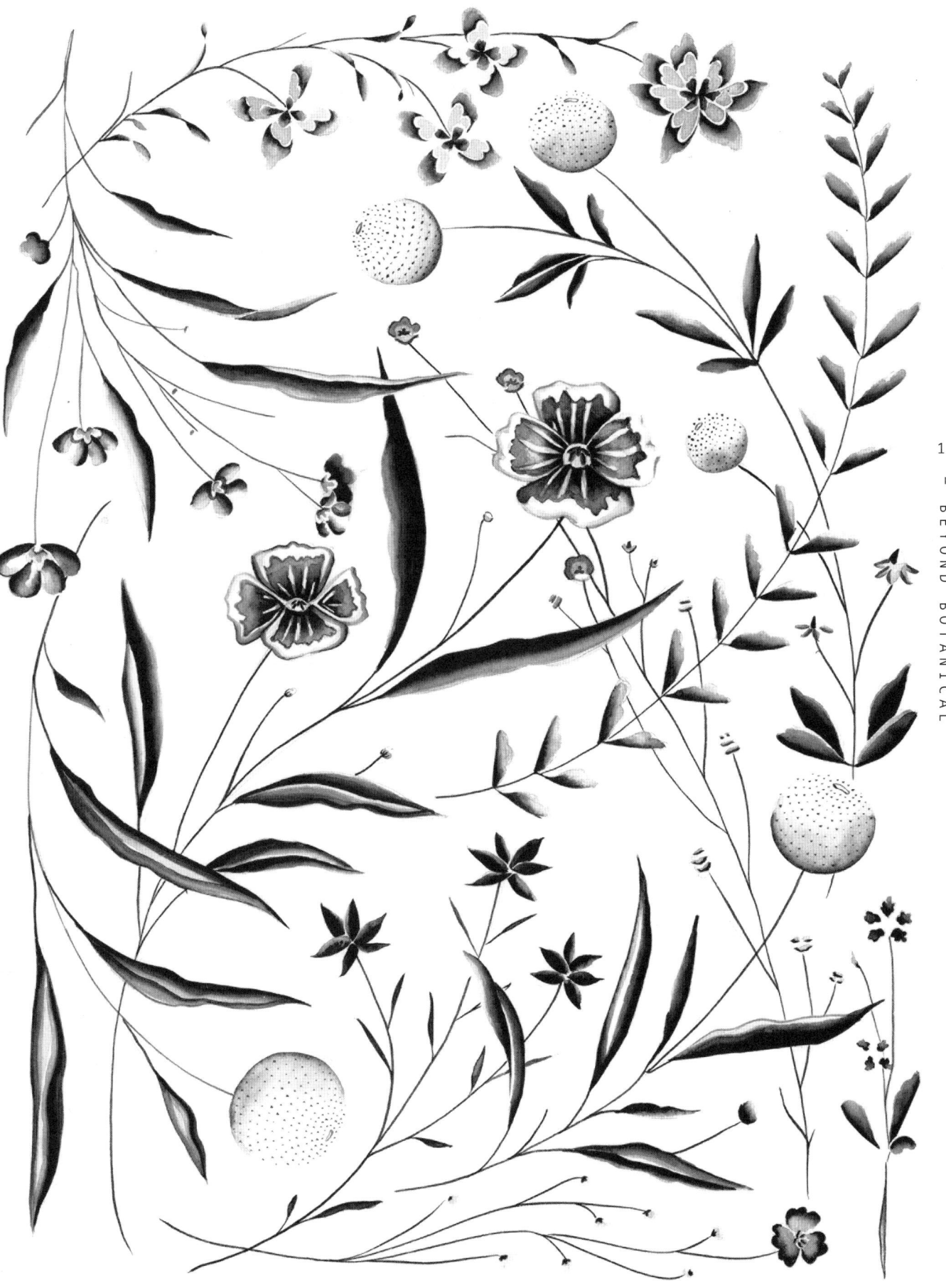

TOUCH, SCENT AND MOTION

A plant is more than what meets the eye: its scent, texture and subtle movement it evokes shape our experience. The roughness of bark or the softness of a petal both influence the way we choose to represent it.

Beyond what you see, what you touch, smell and even hear adds depth to your work. Observe how light filters through leaves, feel the texture of a stem and notice the scent of a flower lingering in the air. Letting these sensory impressions guide your creative process will help you bring more than just accuracy to your drawings.

Equally important to what we sense is what we choose to show, and not every detail needs to appear in your illustration. Maybe you want to highlight the curling edges of a leaf rather than its overall shape, focus on the twisting form of a vine rather than the flowers it carries, or represent the way a bud holds its shape before unfurling. Your choices direct the viewer's attention and tell a story about how you relate to the plants around you.

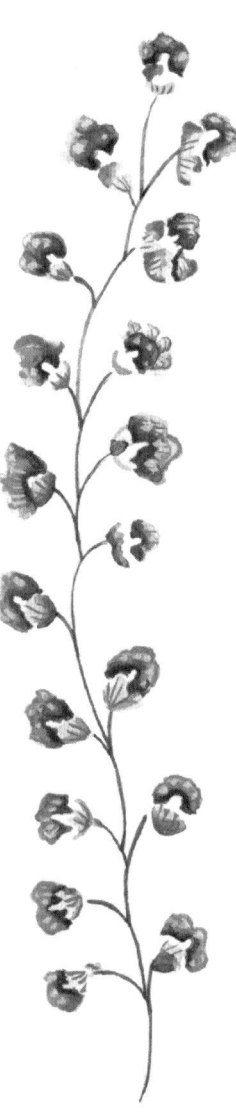

HOW DO YOU FEEL WHEN SURROUNDED BY PLANTS?

_____

_____

_____

_____

_____

_____

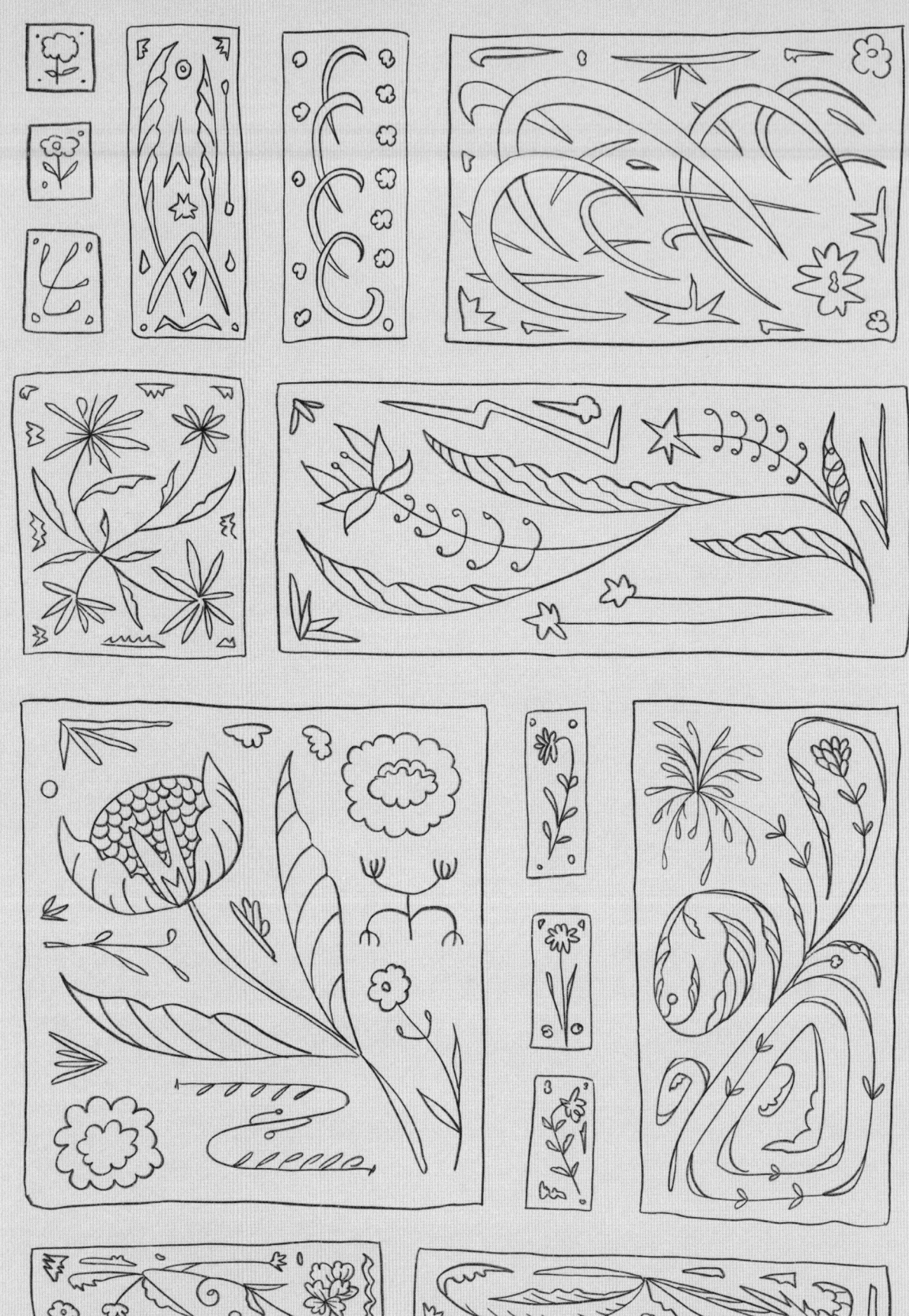

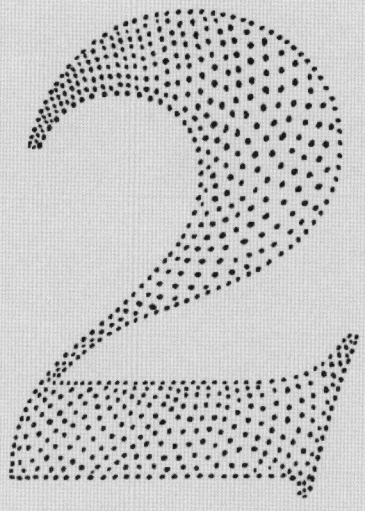

FINDING YOUR WAY THROUGH TOOLS, TECHNIQUES AND SELF-EXPRESSION

Drawing begins in the dialogue between your vision and the materials you use.

In this chapter, we'll explore how different materials influence the way plants land on your page and how experimenting with different approaches can help you develop a style of drawing that feels truly yours.

THE ENTRY GATE

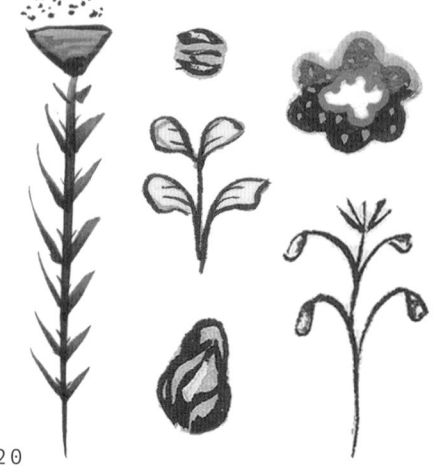

Oftentimes we have an idea in our heads, yet when it reaches the page it doesn't quite match what we envisioned. We might imagine a soft, delicate curve and end up with a shaky line. This is the challenge every artist faces - and what drives us to keep pushing forward.

This gap between vision and execution is something we all experience, and the only way to bridge it is by learning to control the tools and techniques we use, and by having a clear picture of what we want to represent and how to express it. To do this requires consistent practice, paired with an understanding of the materials and techniques that allow us to achieve the results we're aiming for.

In time, the distance between vision and creation becomes smaller, and your drawings begin to carry more of what is truly inside you.

HOW MATERIALS SHAPE OUR EXPERIENCE

The tools you choose shape how you draw plants, and each medium carries its own emotional weight, influencing not only the look of your work but also the experience of creating it.

A fine-tipped pen allows for delicate details, while a thick brushstroke can feel more expressive. Some materials, such as graphite on smooth paper, glide effortlessly, while others, like charcoal on rough paper, create a distinct tactile experience. Each time you explore a new medium, take a moment to observe your reaction.

Every tool leaves its own mark, and the experience of using them is just as important. Some will feel intuitive right away, while others may take time to get used to. Finding materials that sit naturally in your hands will make illustrating more enjoyable and immersive.

You may find yourself drawn to different media in different moments; there's no need to rush. Let curiosity guide your choices, and enjoy discovering those that make the process right for you. Understanding your response to different styles and mediums will help you make intentional choices and bring greater clarity to your work.

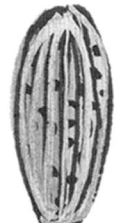
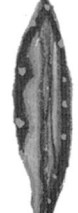
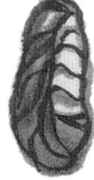
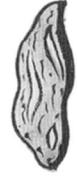
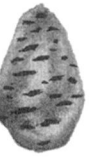
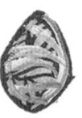

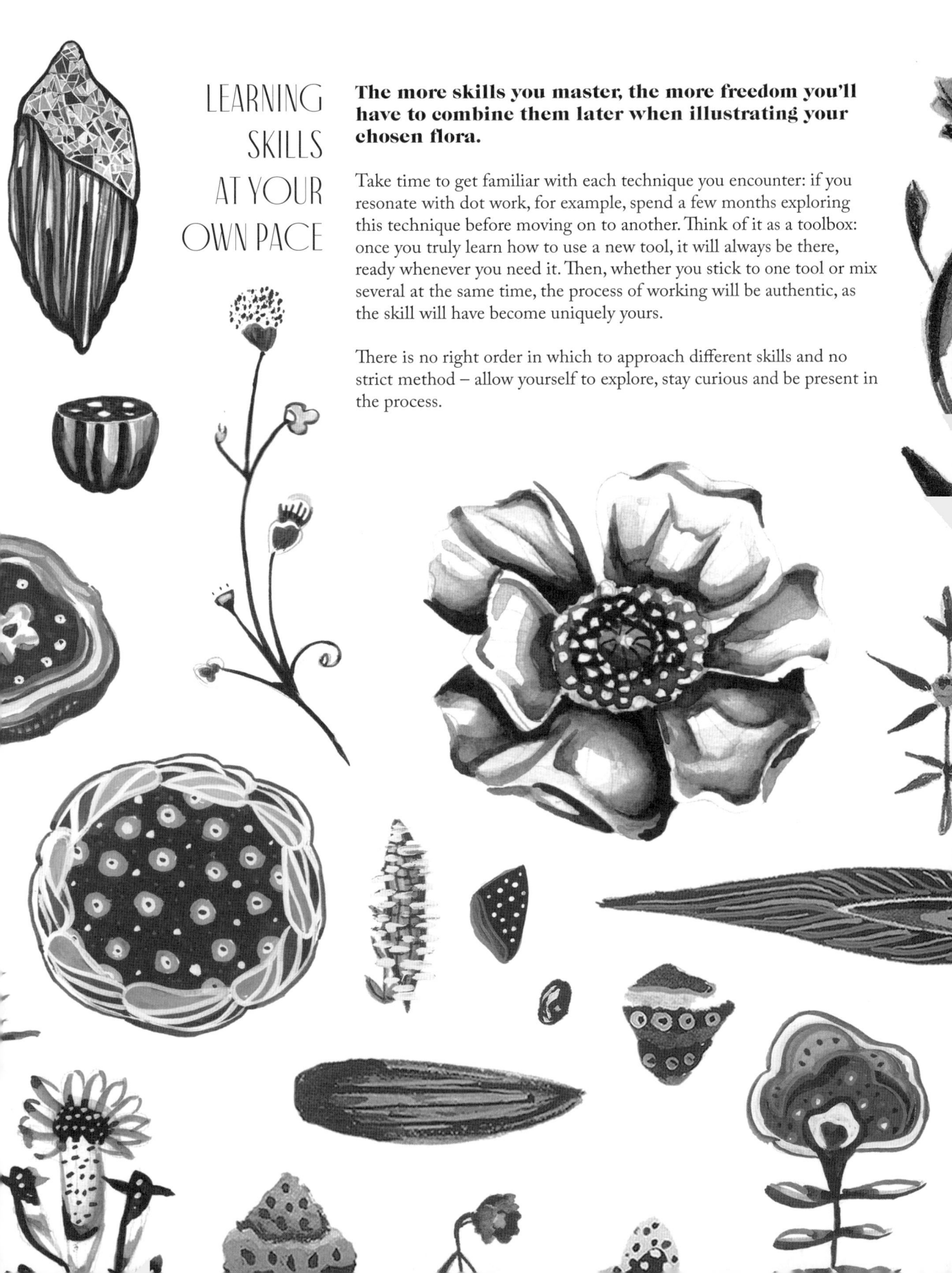

LEARNING SKILLS AT YOUR OWN PACE

The more skills you master, the more freedom you'll have to combine them later when illustrating your chosen flora.

Take time to get familiar with each technique you encounter: if you resonate with dot work, for example, spend a few months exploring this technique before moving on to another. Think of it as a toolbox: once you truly learn how to use a new tool, it will always be there, ready whenever you need it. Then, whether you stick to one tool or mix several at the same time, the process of working will be authentic, as the skill will have become uniquely yours.

There is no right order in which to approach different skills and no strict method – allow yourself to explore, stay curious and be present in the process.

WARMING UP

To translate your ideas onto paper, it's important to teach your hand to move the way you envision. In this section, warm up by drawing over these organic, flowing shapes. Grab a pencil, pen or any tool that feels right to you.

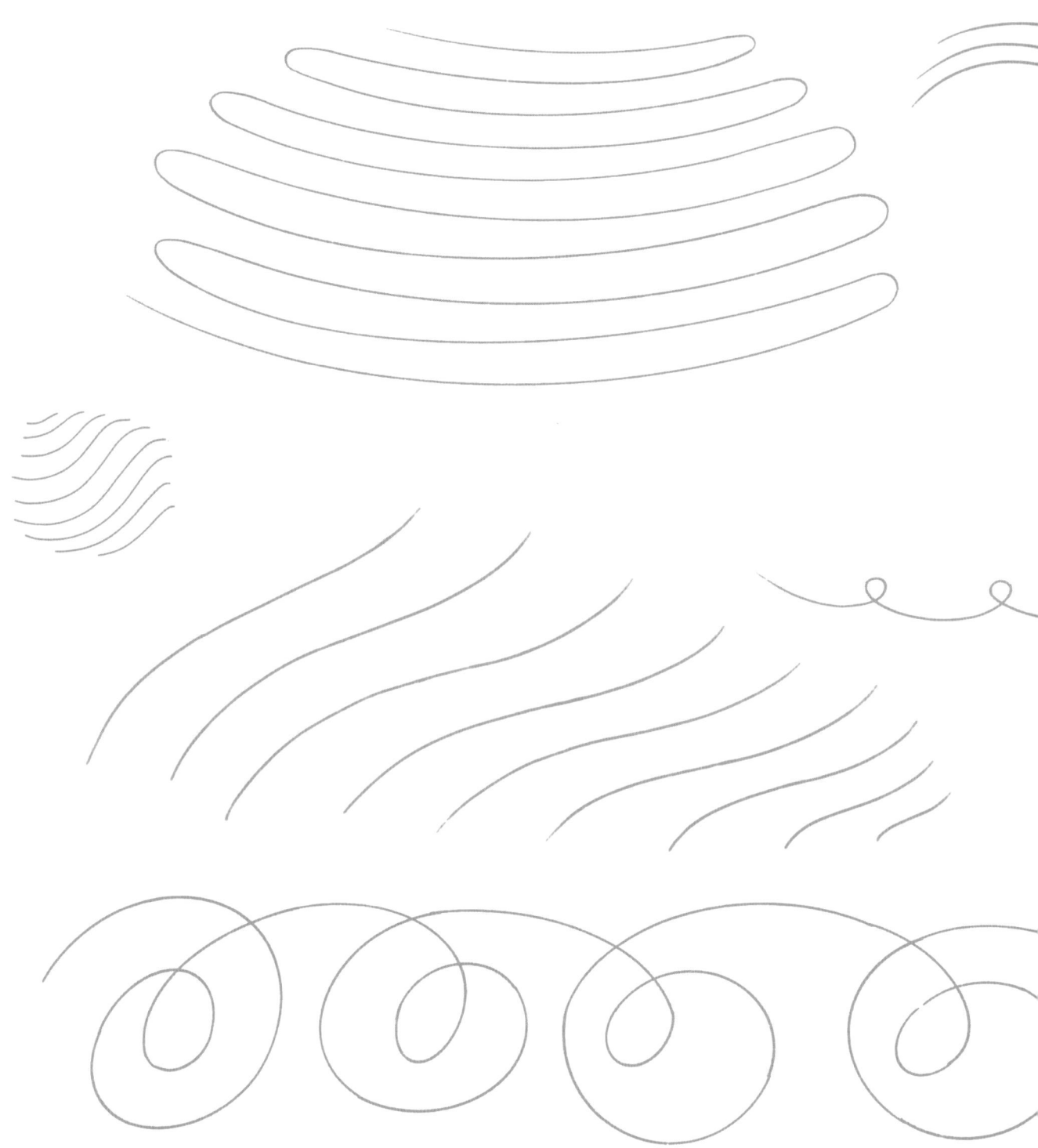

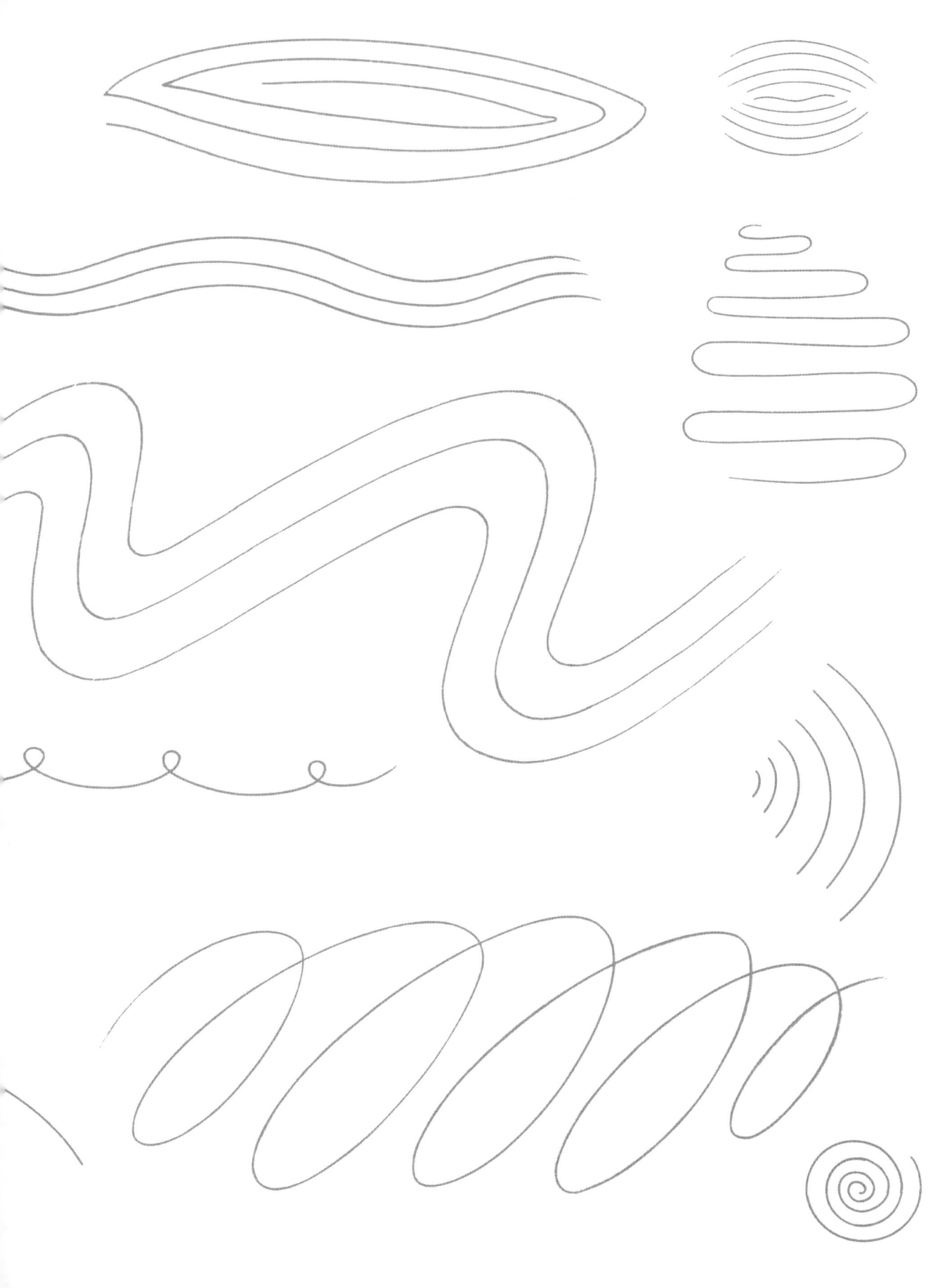

TESTING MATERIALS

Let's try something: choose four different media (for example, pen, pencil, charcoal and crayon). Doodle a bit with each – you might even sketch a small plant or bloom. Beside each doodle, write a few words describing how each medium feels in your hand.

VISUALIZING AND RENDERING

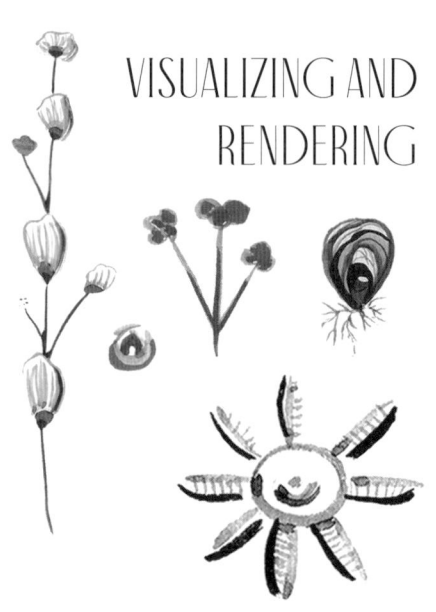

Rendering flowers and plants through drawing and painting can be as simple or as complex as you decide. The possibilities are endless, but keep in mind that complex isn't inherently better than simple.

A single outlined flower can sometimes embody your vision more clearly than a fully shaded one, and both approaches offer their own richness.

Some plants may seem to ask for delicate detail, while others are best captured with loose, expressive strokes. Your approach may shift depending on your mood, the tools you're using or the story you wish to tell.

MIXING IT UP

Give yourself the freedom to experiment - not just with techniques but with how you approach representing plants on paper.

Trying different methods, alternating between materials or even stepping away from a style you've outgrown will all help you refine your practice.

The way you see and depict flora will evolve over time, and that's part of the process. Letting it take its own course is the key to creating images that carry a life of their own.

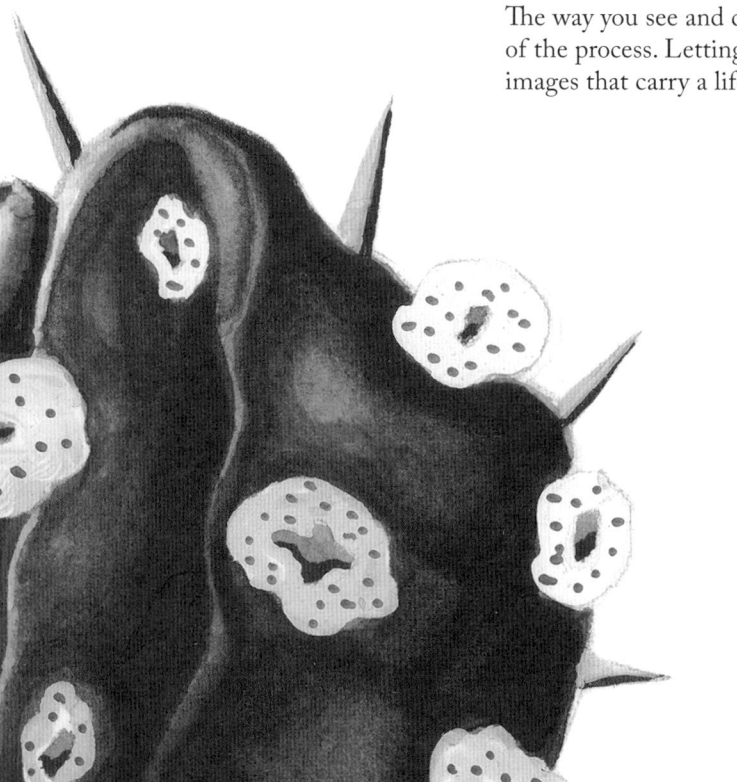

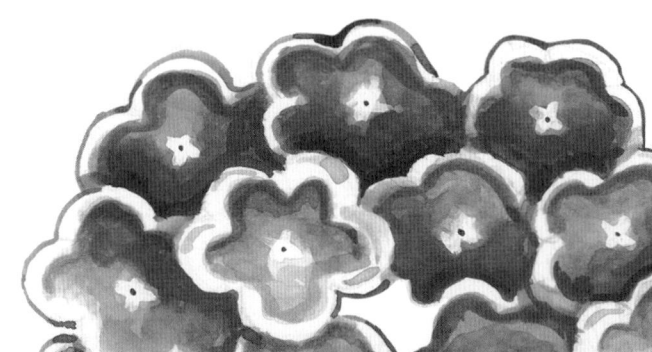

IMAGES THAT FEEL UNIQUE AND TRUE TO YOURSELF

The way you experience the world is already woven into your drawings. Every line carries your gestures, feelings and impressions. When you draw from this awareness, your images feel distinct without you ever needing to force it.

Originality grows from within. It appears naturally when you lean into the way you see, the details you pick up on, the tools you enjoy and the subjects you return to. Other artists can spark ideas and offer inspiration, but their way will always be theirs, just as yours will always be yours.

Sometimes a process or technique feels so resonant that it's worth staying with for a while. A set of materials, a way of mark-making or a theme you keep circling back to can all open new discoveries when given time. If you switch too quickly between approaches, you may miss the depth each one can reveal.

Your individual style will unfold at its own pace. Paying attention to what feels good to create is enough. Your uniqueness is present in every movement of your hand.

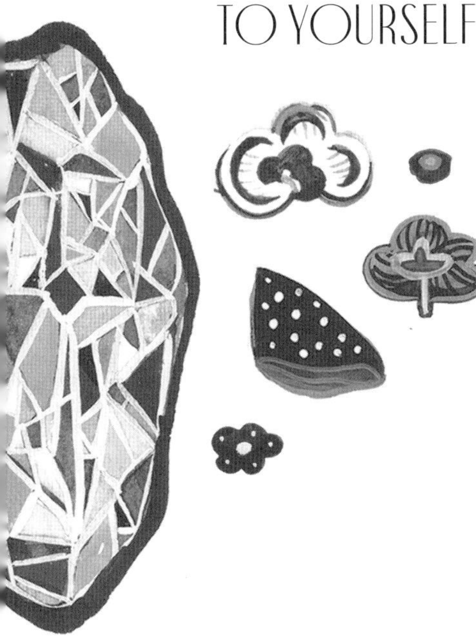

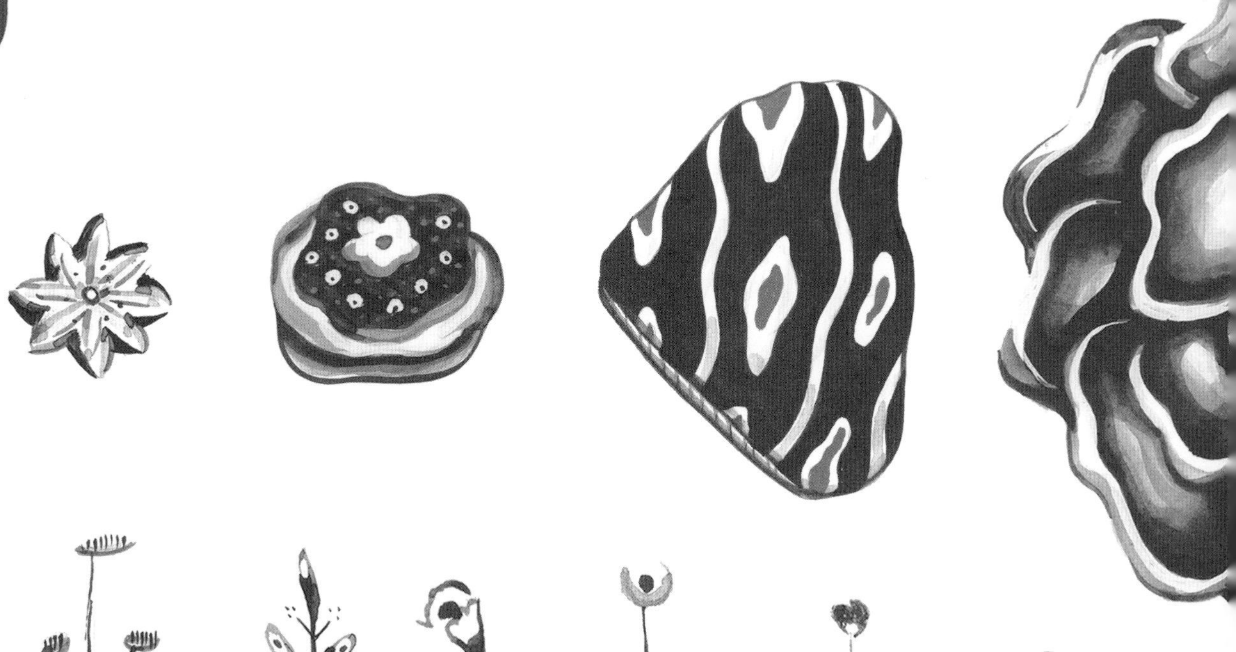

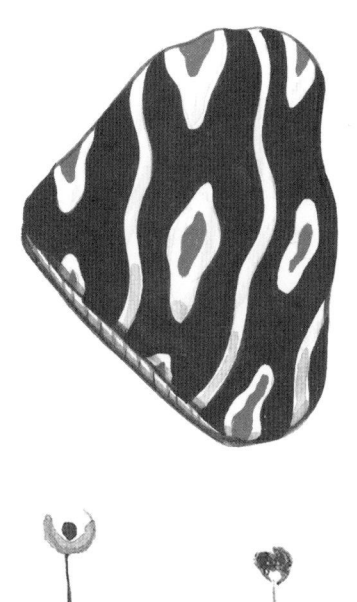

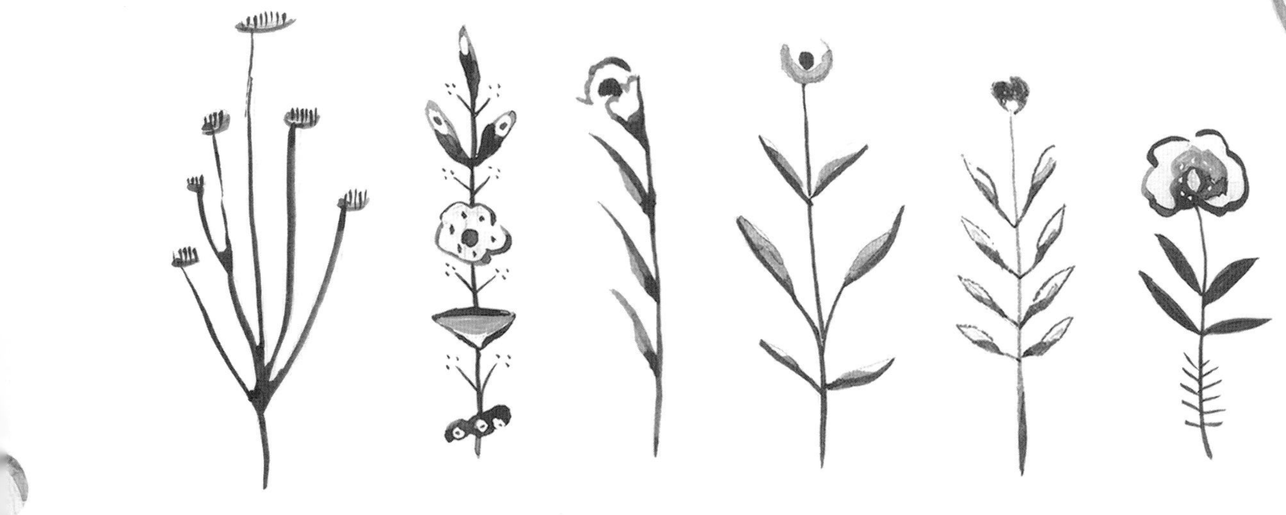

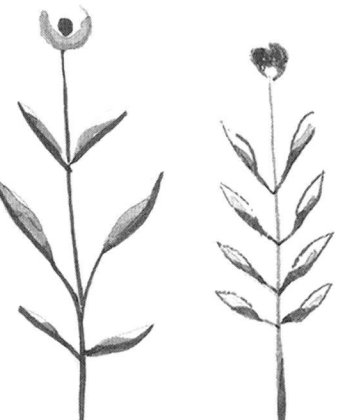

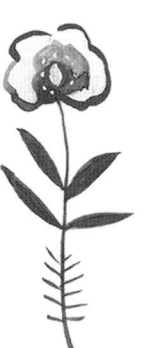

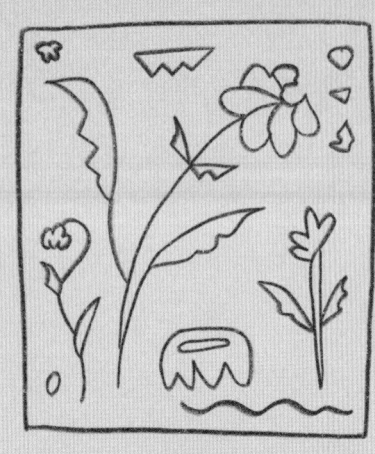
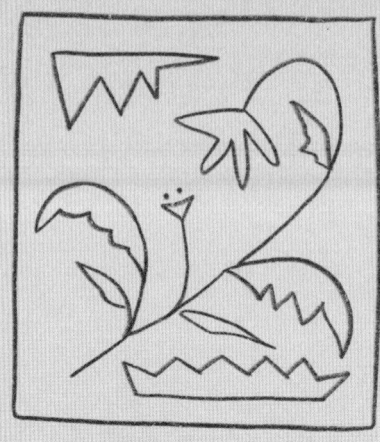
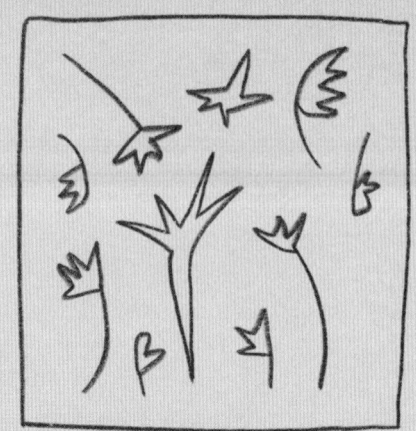
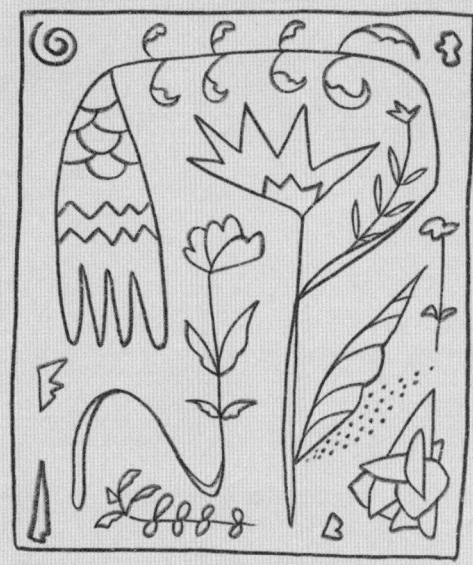
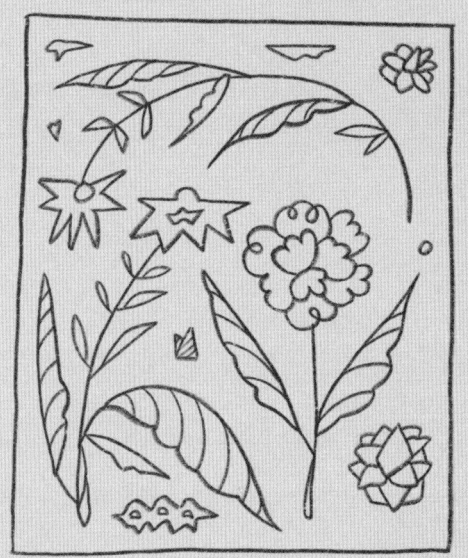
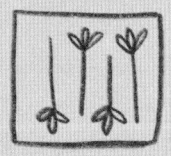
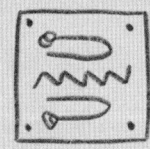
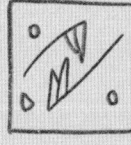
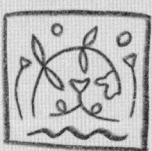
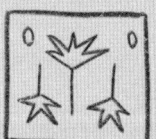
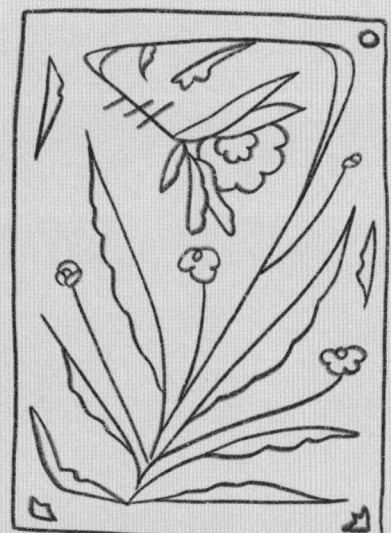
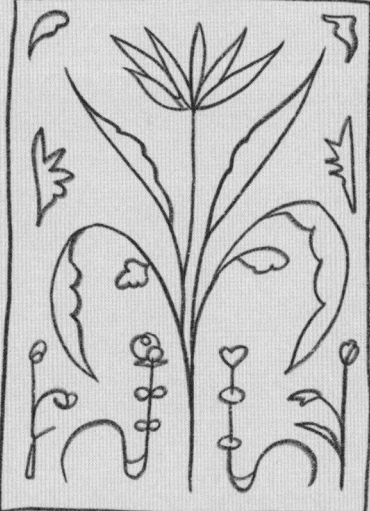
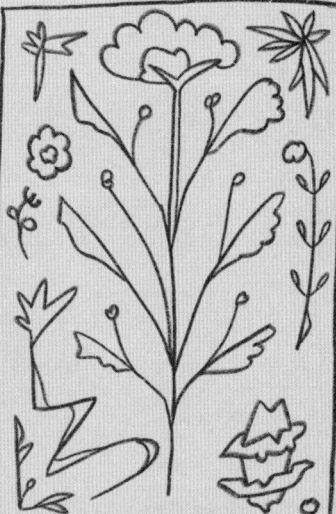

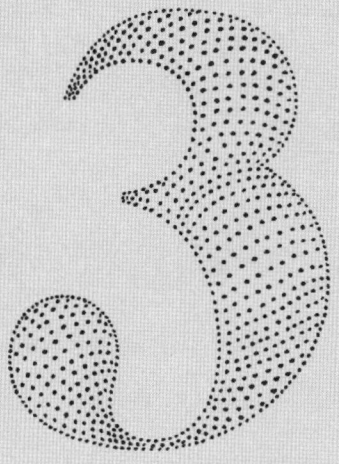

PLANTS AND WHERE
TO FIND THEM

Plants cross our paths in countless forms.

Whether outside, at home or even through the eyes of others, each of these moments is an open door for you to look closer and gather inspiration.

In this chapter, we'll examine how such contexts can shape your drawings and expand on how you translate them onto the page.

INDOORS: LEARNING FROM THE PLANTS YOU LIVE WITH

The plants you grow at home are often the ones you know best. You learn how much light they need, when to water them and how they change through the seasons. For many who live in cities, home is also where the most intimate relationships with plants begin.

Think about what draws you to a particular plant. It might be how its flowers appear at a certain time of year, the slow-motion sequence of a leaf growing day by day or the way light casts shadows across it at a particular moment. Noticing these details deepens your sense of what inspires you in each plant and can feed ideas for future compositions.

OUTDOORS: OBSERVING PLANTS IN THEIR NATURAL HABITAT

Going on a hike, camping or simply lying on the ground in a forest immerses you in plants' true context. Time outdoors not only introduces you to site-specific flora but also helps you learn about the environment and the forces that shape plant growth.

Step into a green space and take a moment to look around. Take in the shifting scents around you. Touch the soil with your hands. Notice the moisture in the air, the movement of insects as they shape their surroundings and the sounds of nature. You may begin a sketch on site and finish it later – in that scenario, try to hold on to those first impressions: the feeling of the place, the atmosphere, the small details that stood out. Even after you leave, let those memories guide your illustrations.

BOTANIC GARDENS: EXPLORING LIVING COLLECTIONS

Walking through a botanic garden surrounds you with an extraordinary variety of forms, textures and species, many of which you wouldn't encounter in your local landscape.

Unlike wild spaces, these gardens bring plants together from across the world into one place, often grouped by region, habitat or use. This setting lets you compare species side by side and notice patterns or relationships that might remain hidden in the wild. You may find yourself drawn to a particular family, an unexpected leaf structure or a flower that blooms only under certain conditions. Let these collected impressions become part of your creative process.

PHOTOGRAPHY: DOCUMENTING PLANTS FOR REFERENCE

Sometimes a plant catches your attention and a photograph is the one tool available to hold onto it. Taking pictures is useful for reference, but remember that cameras can flatten depth and distort scale.

If possible, pause before you take the photo. Observe the plant closely: touch its surface, notice its scent and the way the light falls on it. The more you engage in that moment, the easier it will be to recall when you look at the image later.

Photographs don't always capture every detail you might need. If you come across an unfamiliar plant, searching for more images online or in books can help you understand its structure, growth patterns and variations. Each photograph adds another layer of reference, extending the impressions you gathered in the moment.

MUSEUMS AND EXHIBITIONS: LEARNING FROM OTHER ARTISTS

Throughout history, artists have represented flowers in countless ways, each offering a different perspective and revealing unique aspects of the flora around us.

Observing the compositions and techniques of others can open possibilities that may inspire your next work. By paying attention to the decisions behind their artwork, you start to notice more options in your own. Visiting exhibitions or museums can broaden your perception even further, giving you the chance to see how different artists across time and place have approached the same subject.

WHERE COULD YOU GO TO MEET PLANTS NEAR YOU?

FIELD NOTES: EXPLORING NEW ENVIRONMENTS

Whether walking in a forest or visiting a botanic garden, be conscious of the space around you - the ground beneath, the air moving through it, the living world it holds. This is the environment that nurtures the plants you'll be spending time with. Grab your sketching tools, some snacks and water, and set out to discover unfamiliar plants.

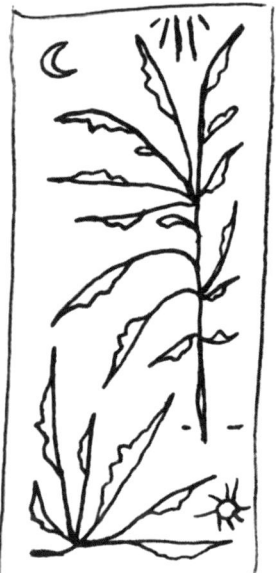

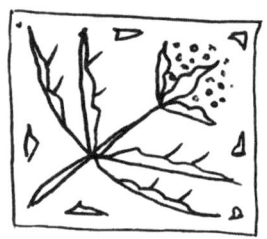

Instead of stopping at the first plant that catches your attention, wander a little. Draw a page of small shapes and, without overthinking, fill them with quick doodles of the details that catch your eye. It could be the structure of a flower, a withered leaf or a pattern you've never seen before … any sort of impression, as if you are drifting through the space around you. Use whatever materials feel comfortable and enjoy the process.

When your page is full, step back and look at it as a whole. Together, the doodles should feel like a small gallery of observations – a microcosm of the environment around you. From here, you can choose which plants you'd like to spend more time with. This is the moment where your drawing session begins, moving from quick impressions into slower, closer observation.

Add notes – such as the day, location, season, temperature – and any observations you want to keep, so you can link the sketches to the moment you experienced them.

Over time, these pages will gather into a sketchbook of places you have visited, each one a source of inspiration for your future botanical creations. The drawings on these two pages are from one of my visits to Chelsea Physic Garden in London to show you how the exercise works. On pages 34–5 you'll also find some space for you to try it yourself – this time, I've drawn the shapes to get you started.

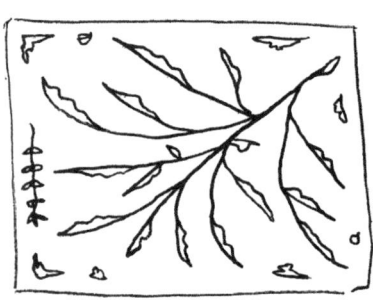

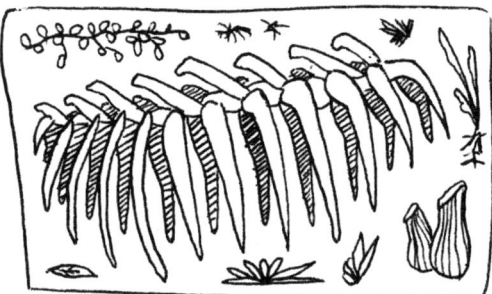

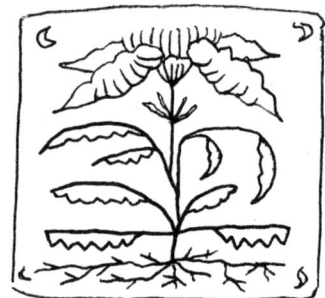

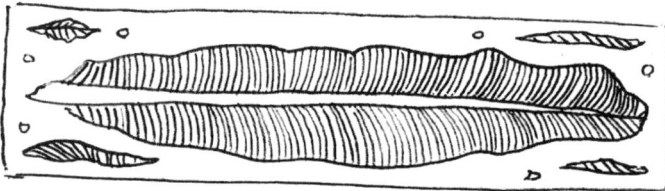

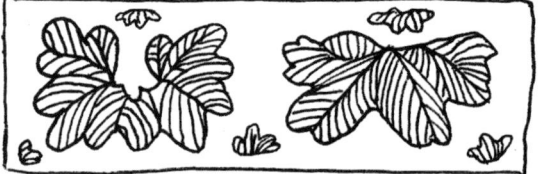

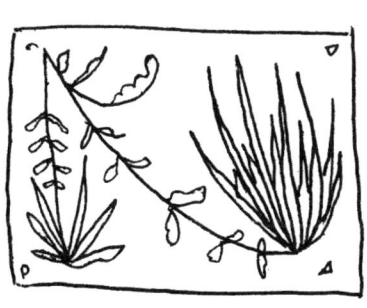
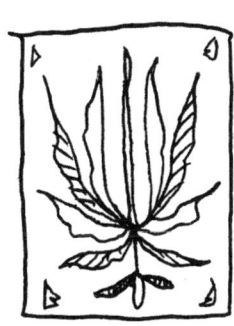
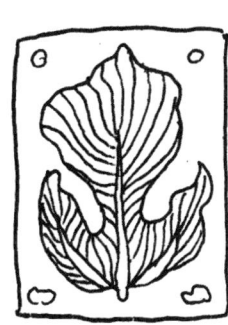
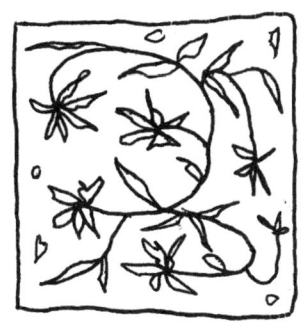
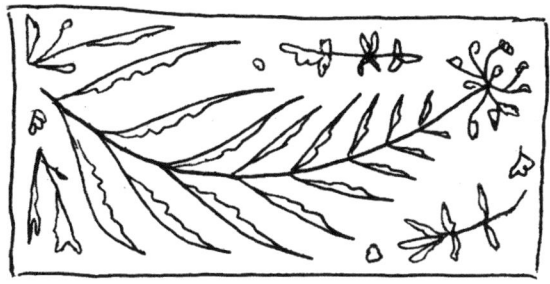
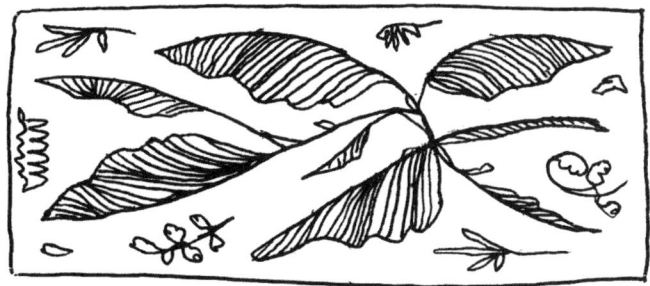
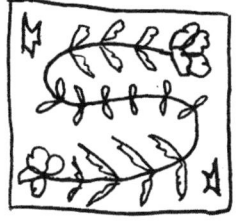
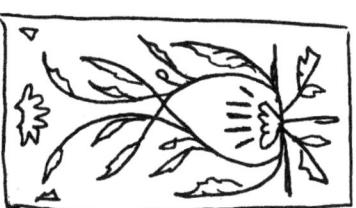
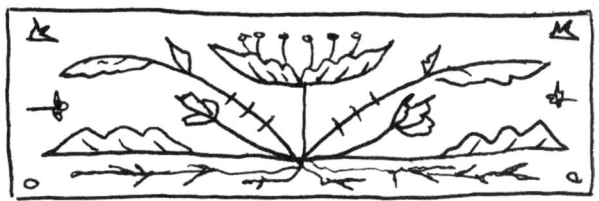
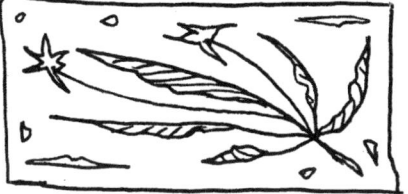
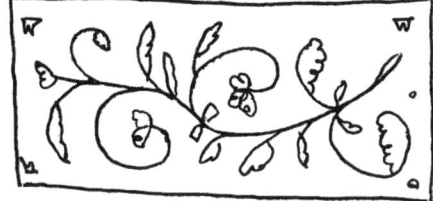
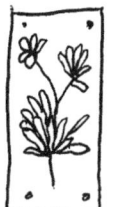
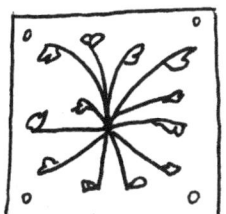
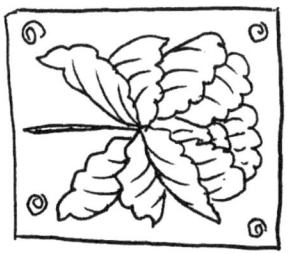
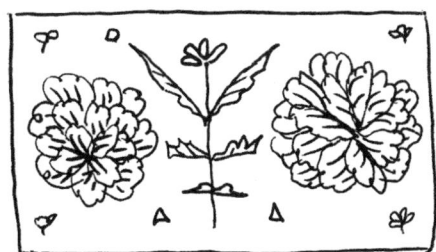
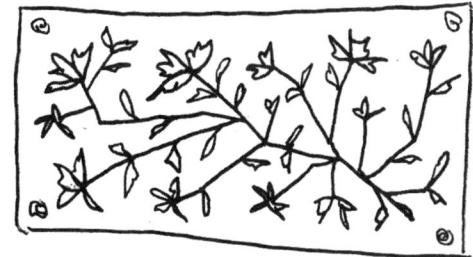
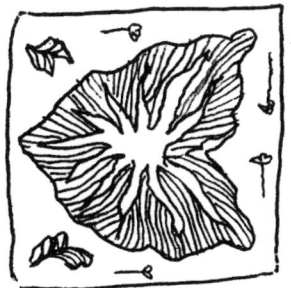
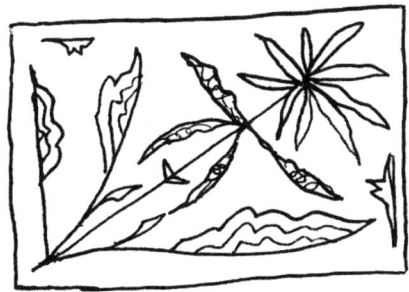
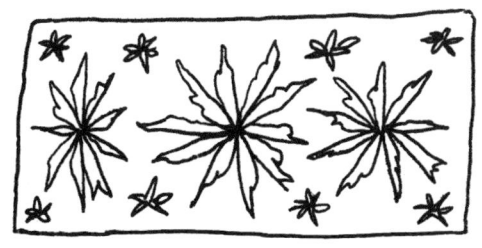

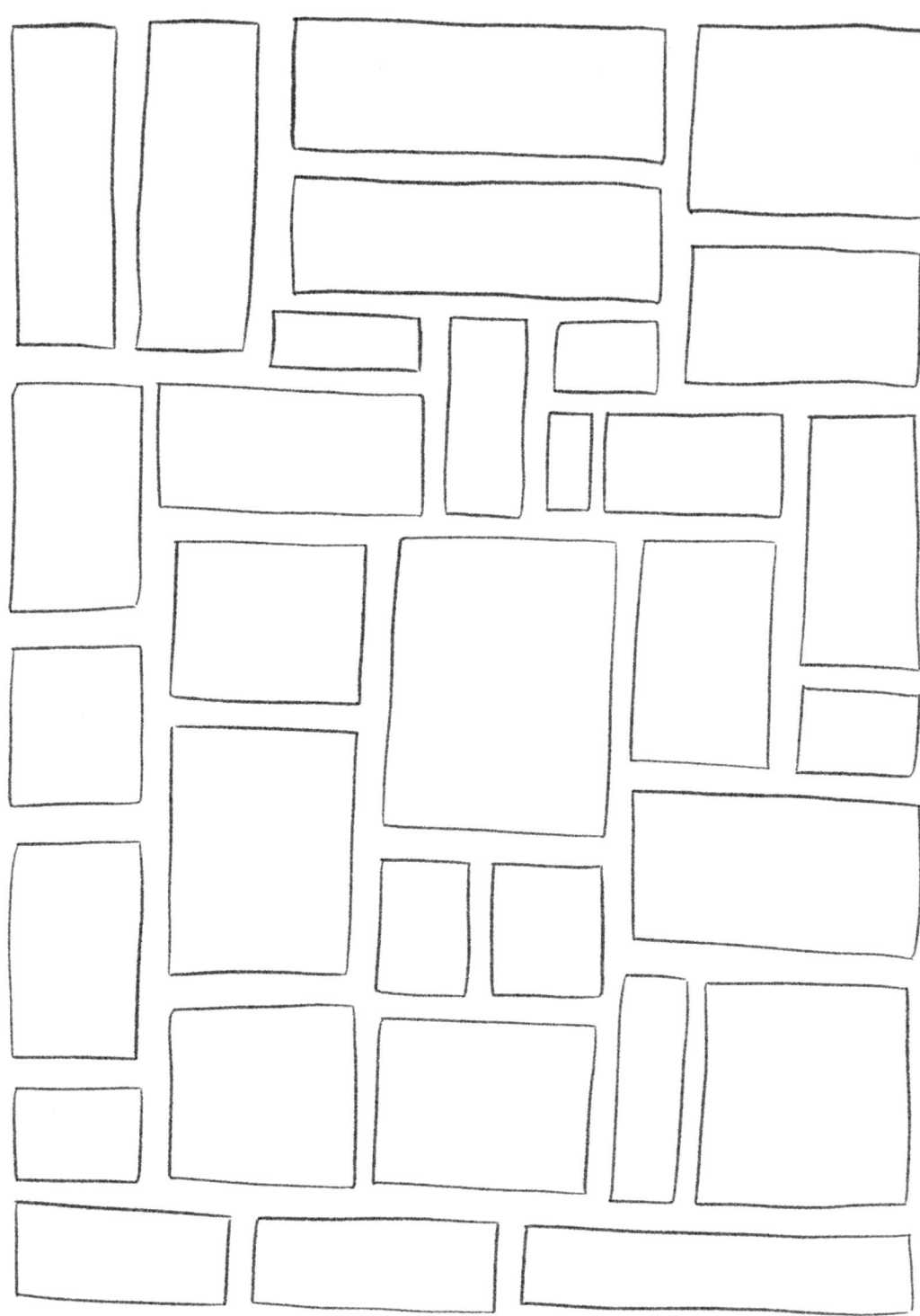

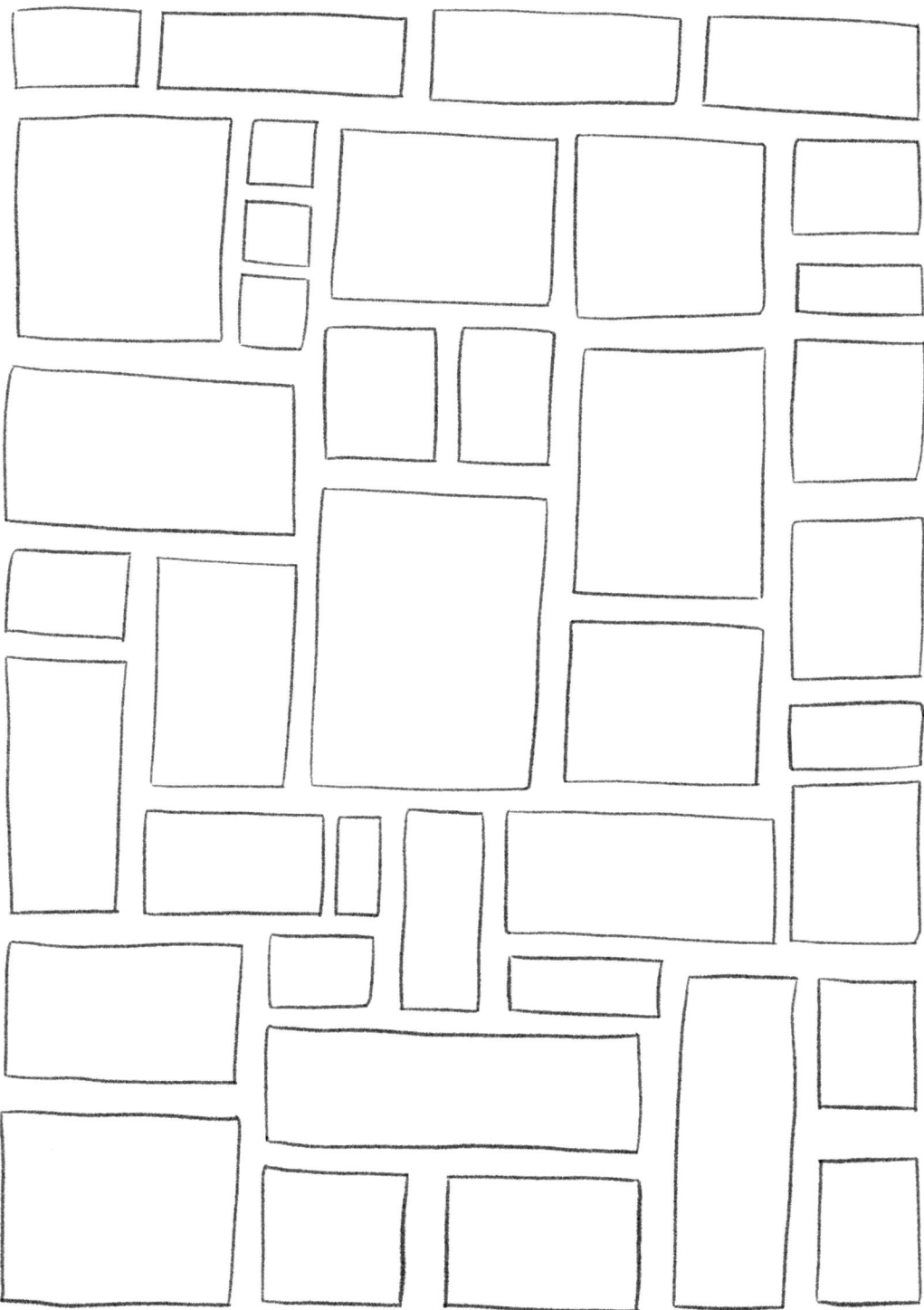

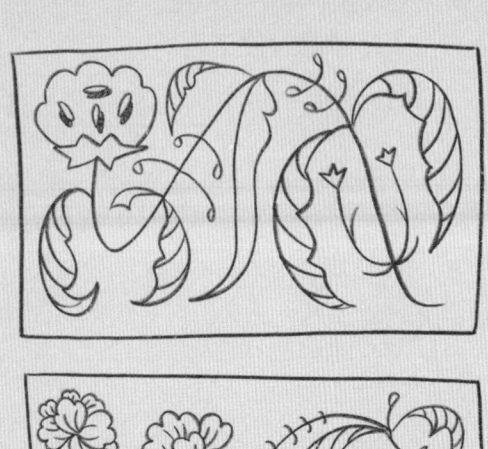
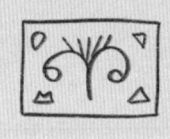
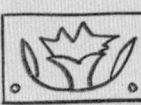
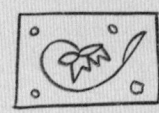

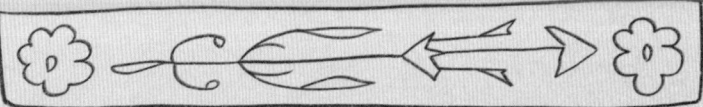
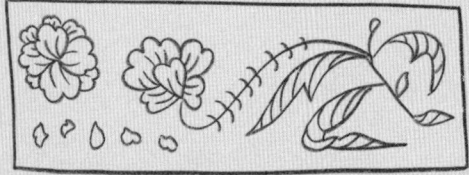
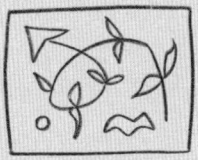
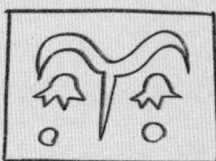
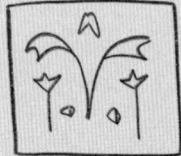
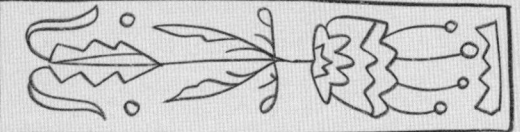
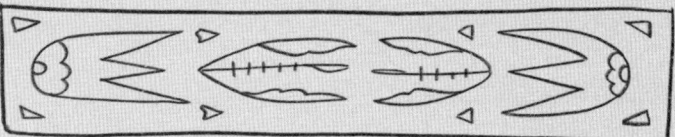
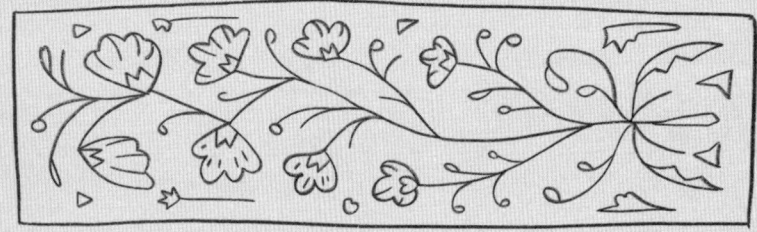
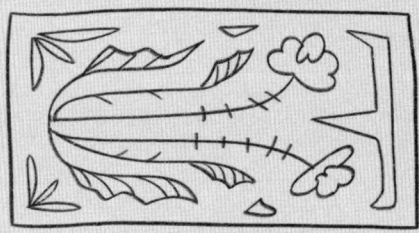
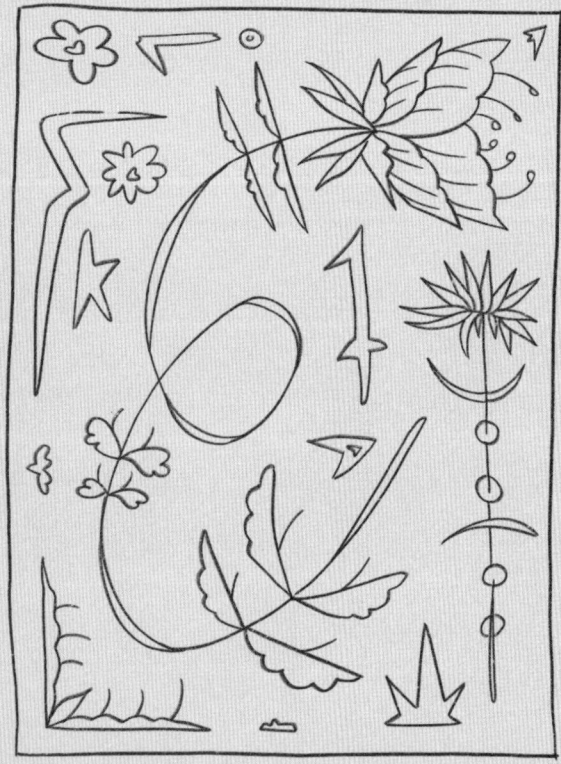
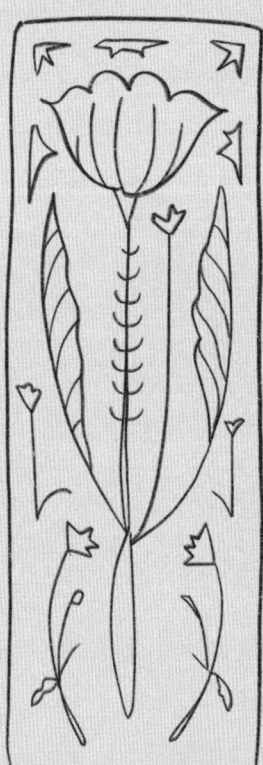
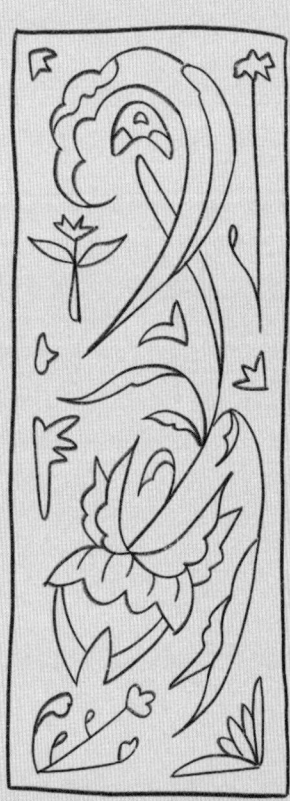

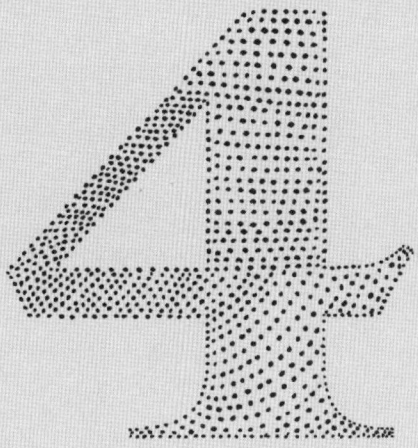

BETWEEN SPACE AND FORM

Behind each botanical illustration are choices about space, depth, light and the natural cycles of plants, all of which shape how your composition feels.

This chapter serves as a sourcebook you can return to, offering guidance and fresh perspectives along the way. Rather than presenting a single 'correct' method to compose, shade or draw with proper proportion, these pages share possibilities and observations to help expand your perception.

You'll discover how shading shifts the mood of a flower, how viewpoint changes the sense of depth and how reflecting on plant cycles can make your compositions feel more natural and alive.

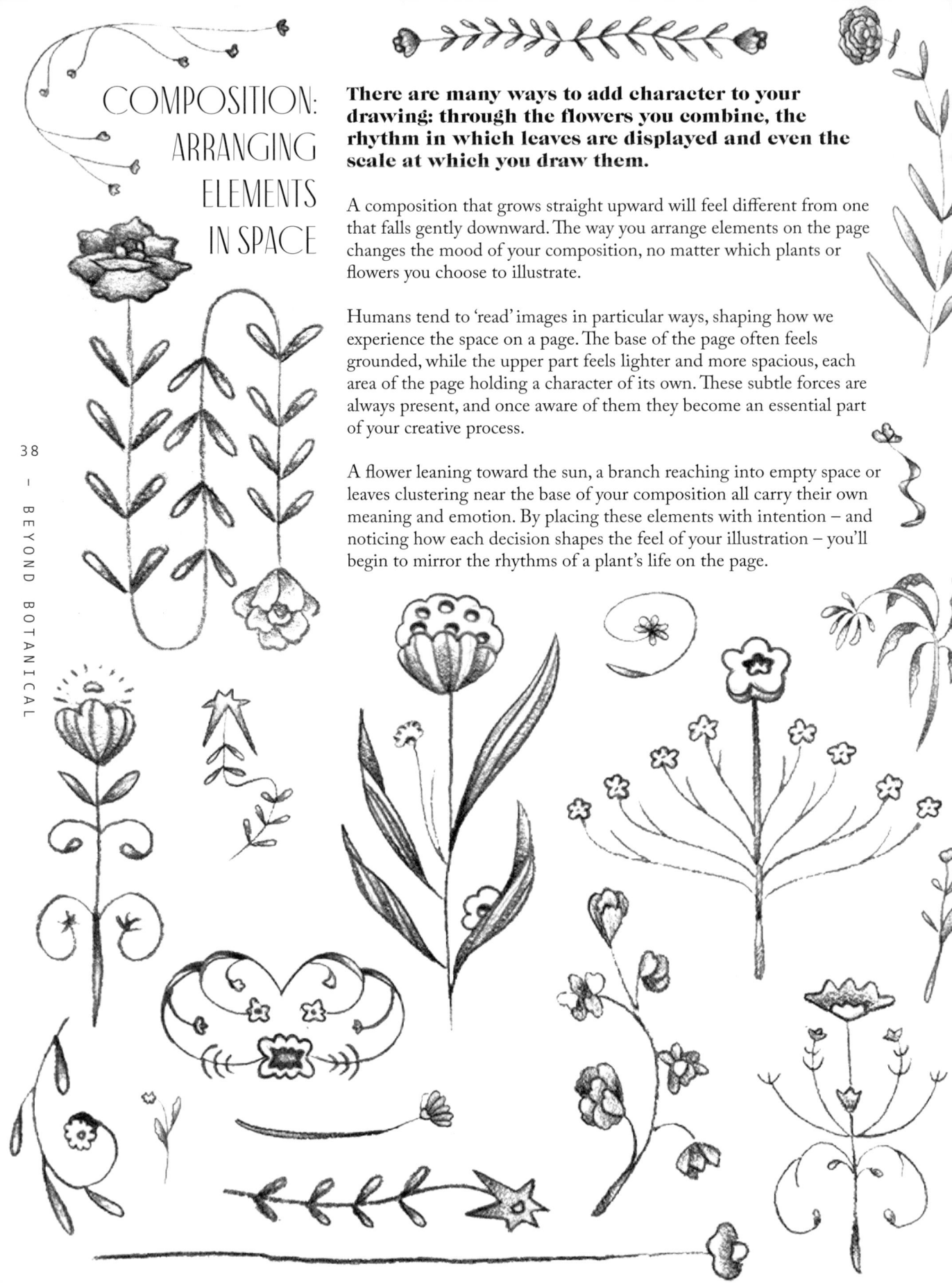

COMPOSITION: ARRANGING ELEMENTS IN SPACE

There are many ways to add character to your drawing: through the flowers you combine, the rhythm in which leaves are displayed and even the scale at which you draw them.

A composition that grows straight upward will feel different from one that falls gently downward. The way you arrange elements on the page changes the mood of your composition, no matter which plants or flowers you choose to illustrate.

Humans tend to 'read' images in particular ways, shaping how we experience the space on a page. The base of the page often feels grounded, while the upper part feels lighter and more spacious, each area of the page holding a character of its own. These subtle forces are always present, and once aware of them they become an essential part of your creative process.

A flower leaning toward the sun, a branch reaching into empty space or leaves clustering near the base of your composition all carry their own meaning and emotion. By placing these elements with intention – and noticing how each decision shapes the feel of your illustration – you'll begin to mirror the rhythms of a plant's life on the page.

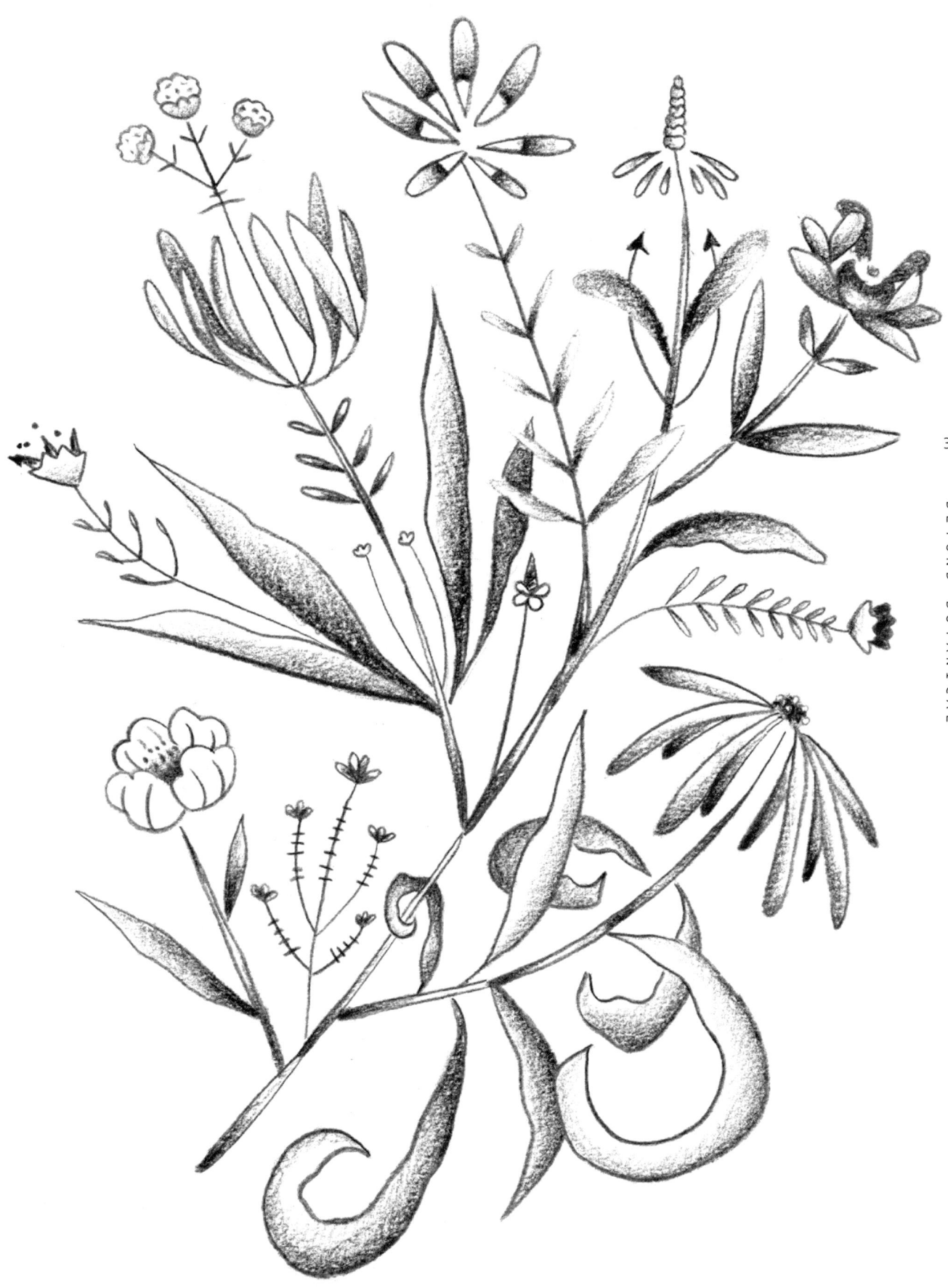

NEGATIVE SPACE: OBSERVING THE UNSEEN

As you draw stems, leaves and flowers, hidden shapes emerge in the spaces around them, carrying as much presence as the lines on the paper. These in-between forms are known as 'negative space', and they naturally appear as you place elements together. One of the best ways to keep your drawing balanced is by acknowledging these subtle shapes as much as the lines themselves.

It might feel challenging at first to keep an eye on both the forms you draw and the openings around them, but with practice it becomes second nature. Squinting at your drawing or flipping it upside down can make these shapes more noticeable and help you see whether your composition feels balanced.

Spaces between stems serve as pauses, breaks that allow the eye to follow the rhythm of the drawing more clearly. The clearings between clusters of leaves can act like pathways, leading the eye across the page. Negative space also shapes the structure of a composition and heightens the presence of each part, making the arrangement feel thoughtful and letting every detail stand out – just like how in music, it's as much about the notes you don't play.

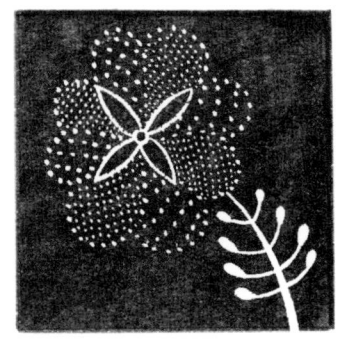

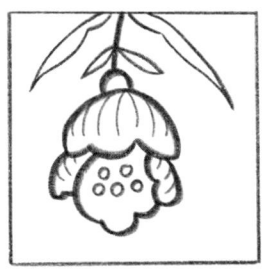
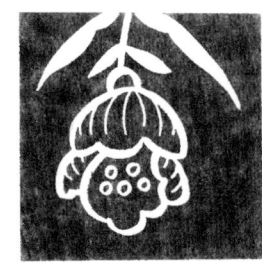
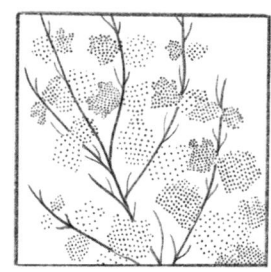
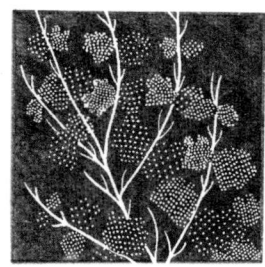

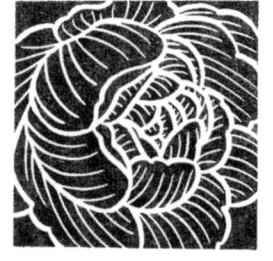
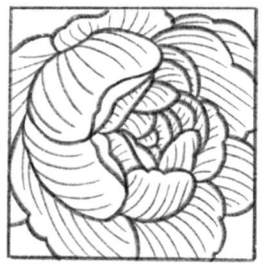

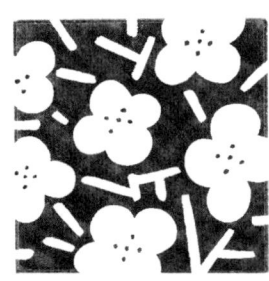

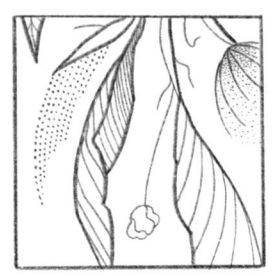
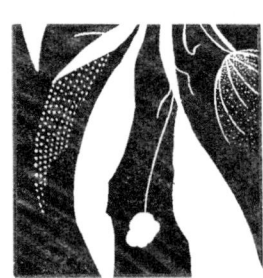
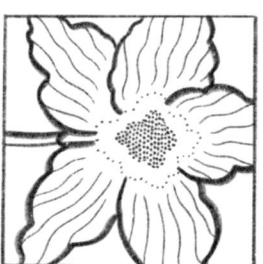
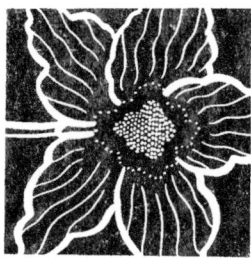

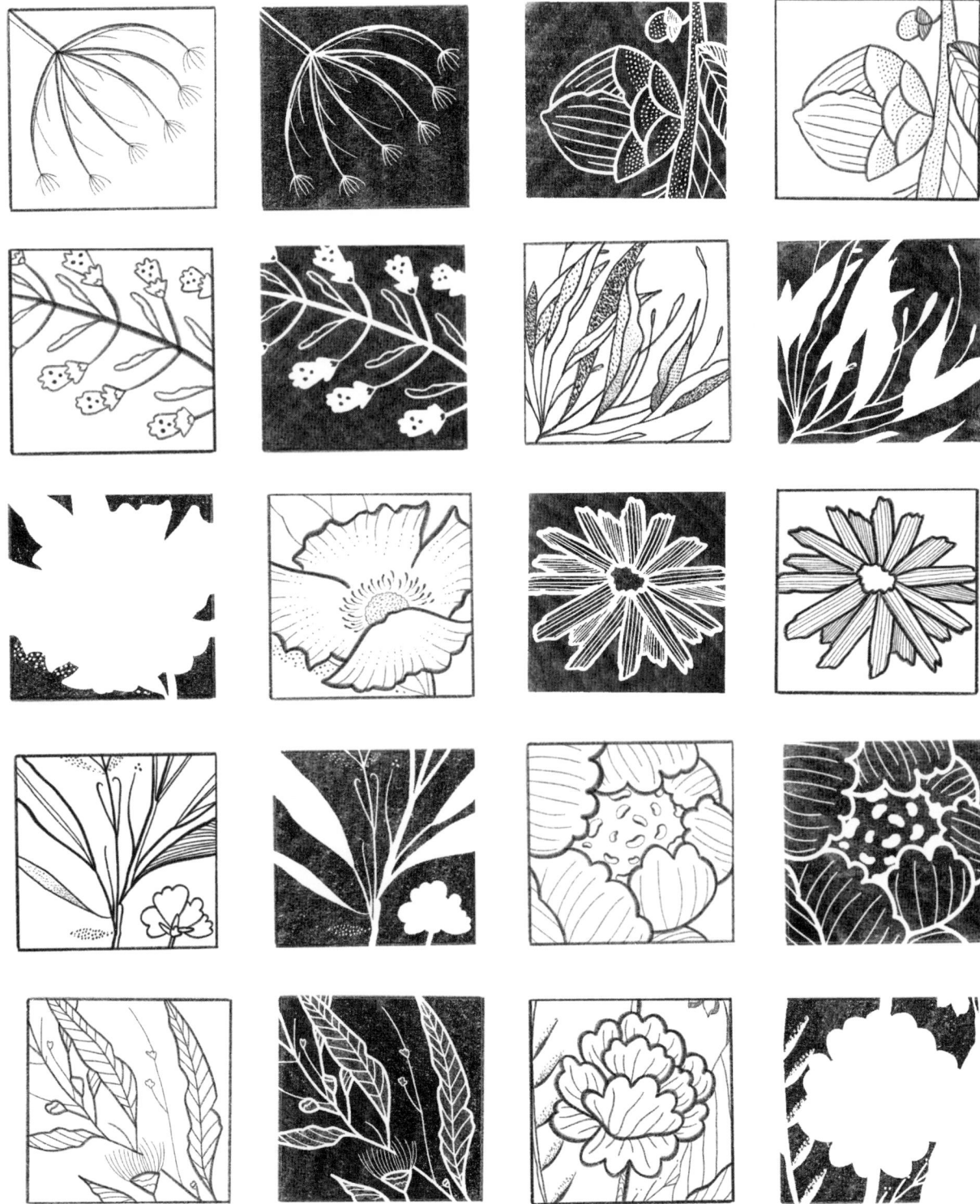

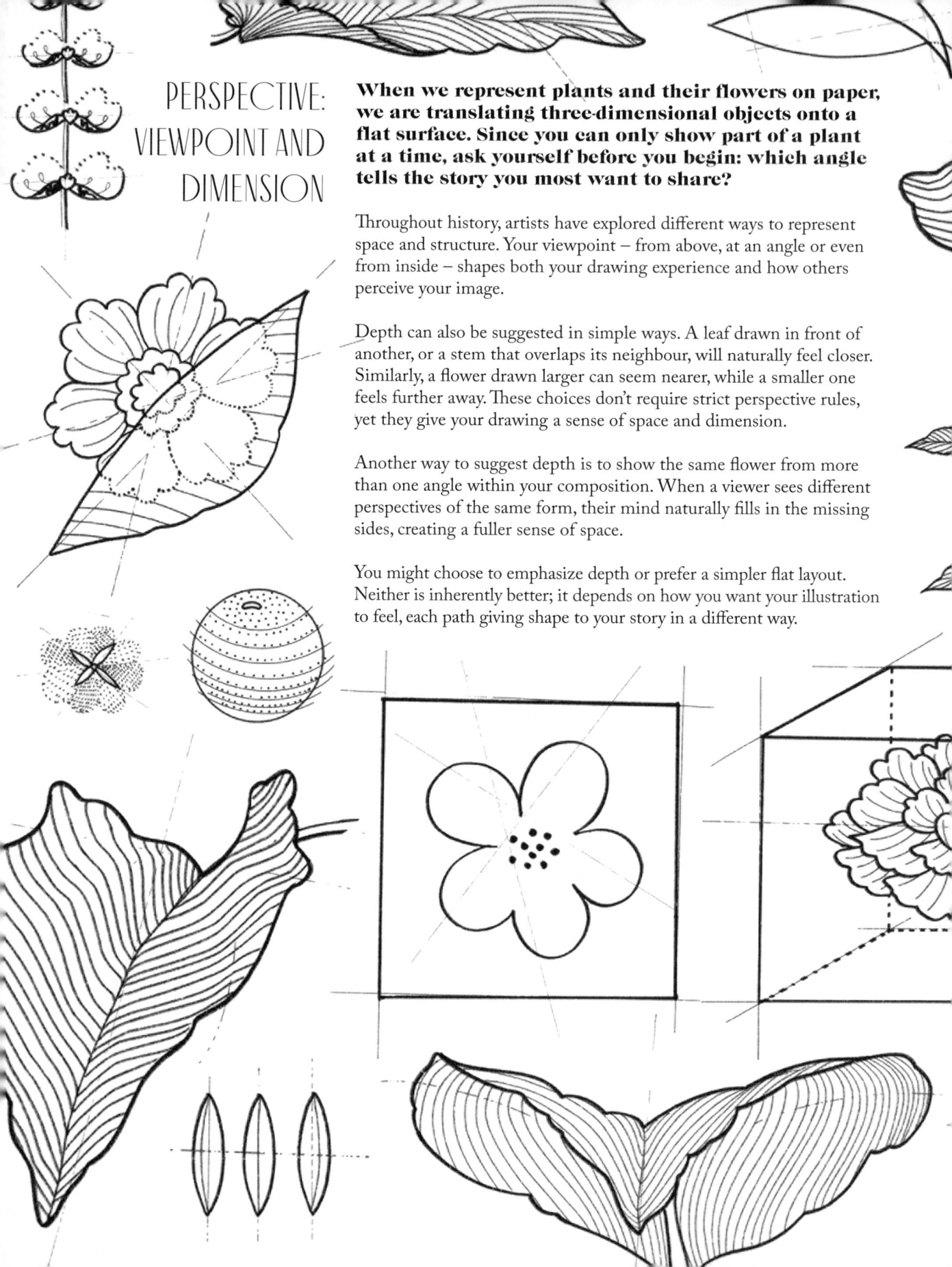

PERSPECTIVE: VIEWPOINT AND DIMENSION

When we represent plants and their flowers on paper, we are translating three-dimensional objects onto a flat surface. Since you can only show part of a plant at a time, ask yourself before you begin: which angle tells the story you most want to share?

Throughout history, artists have explored different ways to represent space and structure. Your viewpoint – from above, at an angle or even from inside – shapes both your drawing experience and how others perceive your image.

Depth can also be suggested in simple ways. A leaf drawn in front of another, or a stem that overlaps its neighbour, will naturally feel closer. Similarly, a flower drawn larger can seem nearer, while a smaller one feels further away. These choices don't require strict perspective rules, yet they give your drawing a sense of space and dimension.

Another way to suggest depth is to show the same flower from more than one angle within your composition. When a viewer sees different perspectives of the same form, their mind naturally fills in the missing sides, creating a fuller sense of space.

You might choose to emphasize depth or prefer a simpler flat layout. Neither is inherently better; it depends on how you want your illustration to feel, each path giving shape to your story in a different way.

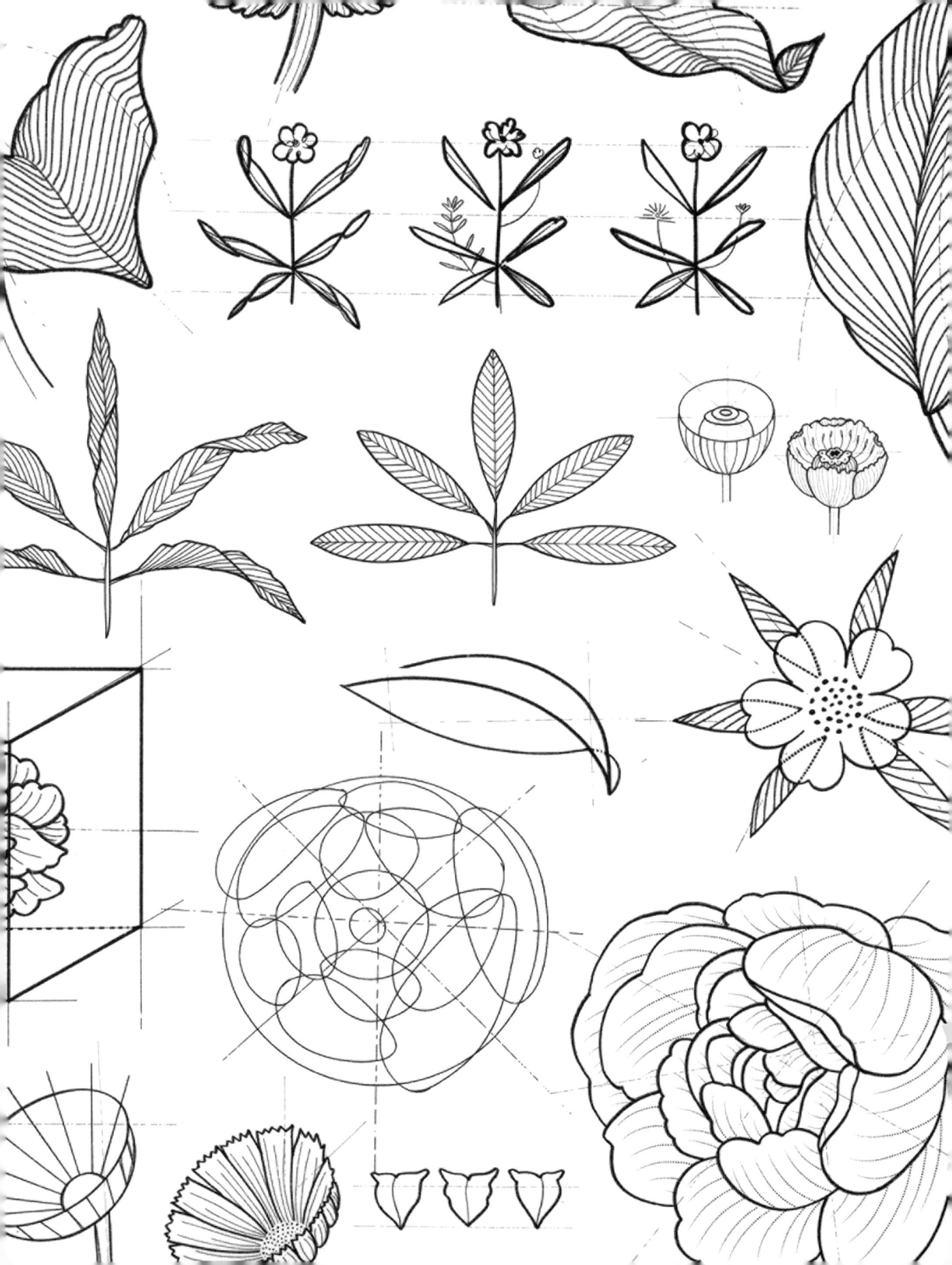

SHADING: LIGHT, DEPTH AND ATMOSPHERE

As you observe plants around you, notice how light lies across every leaf, petal and stem. Through shading you can translate that play of light into your drawing, bringing depth and feeling. Softer tones often suggest a calm, delicate mood, while darker, denser shades can express strength and intensity.

Look at the gentle transitions between light and dark, as these subtle shifts give your drawings volume and depth. Twist a leaf or a flower gently between your fingers, and you'll see how light and shade shift. Notice the texture of each leaf or petal. Smooth, soft surfaces catch light differently from rough or velvety ones. Let your shading follow these qualities, or challenge them to shift the mood of your drawing.

Follow the edges of your shadows. Softer edges make a form appear delicate, while sharper edges give structure and definition. Building up tones slowly allows depth and form to emerge while staying in control of your drawing. With practice, you'll learn to discern values more precisely and decide how dark or light each area needs to be.

Become aware of how leaves, petal and stems cast shadows across each other. The more you study these relationships and experiment with different ways of applying shading, the more specific your choices will become, showing more of your individual self.

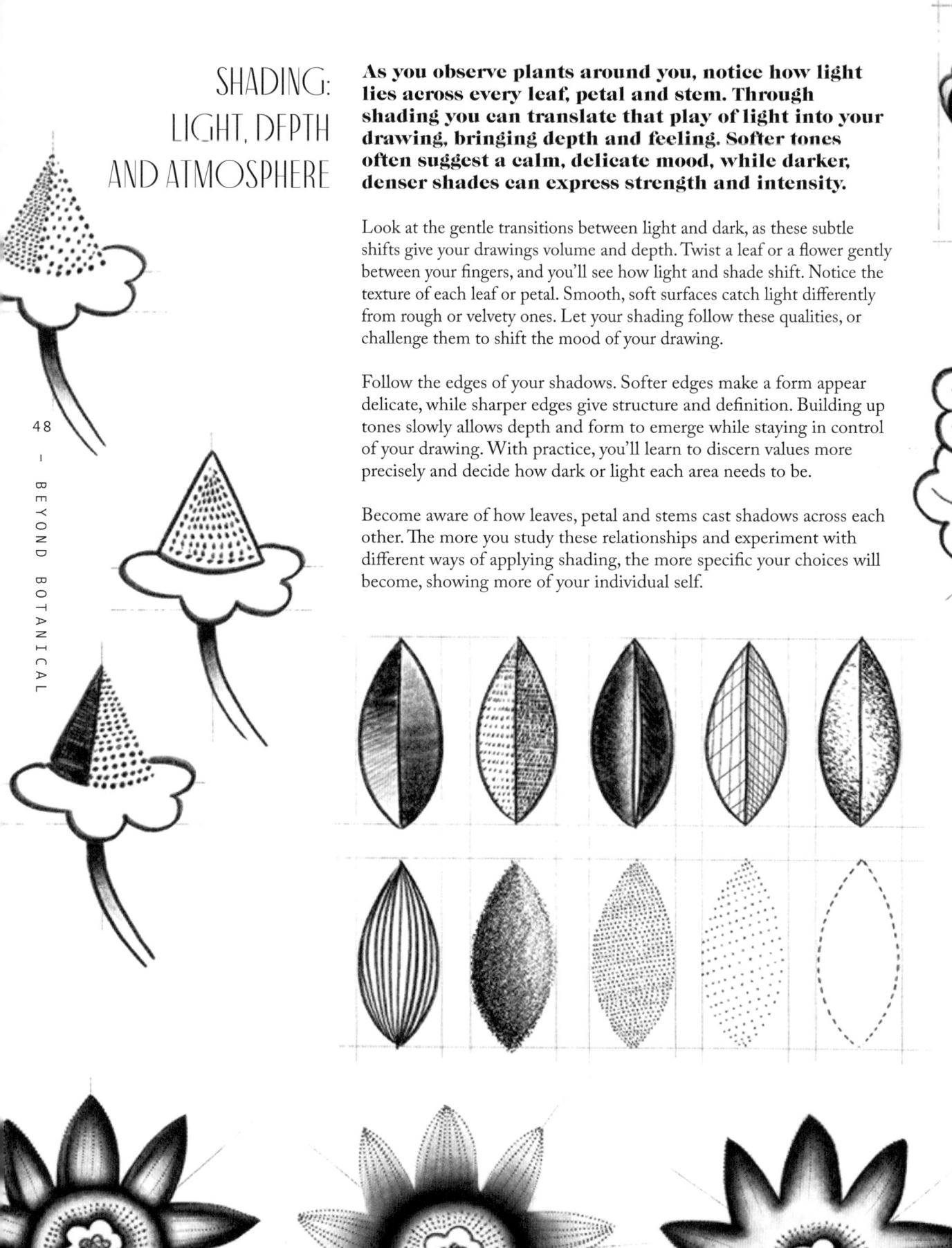

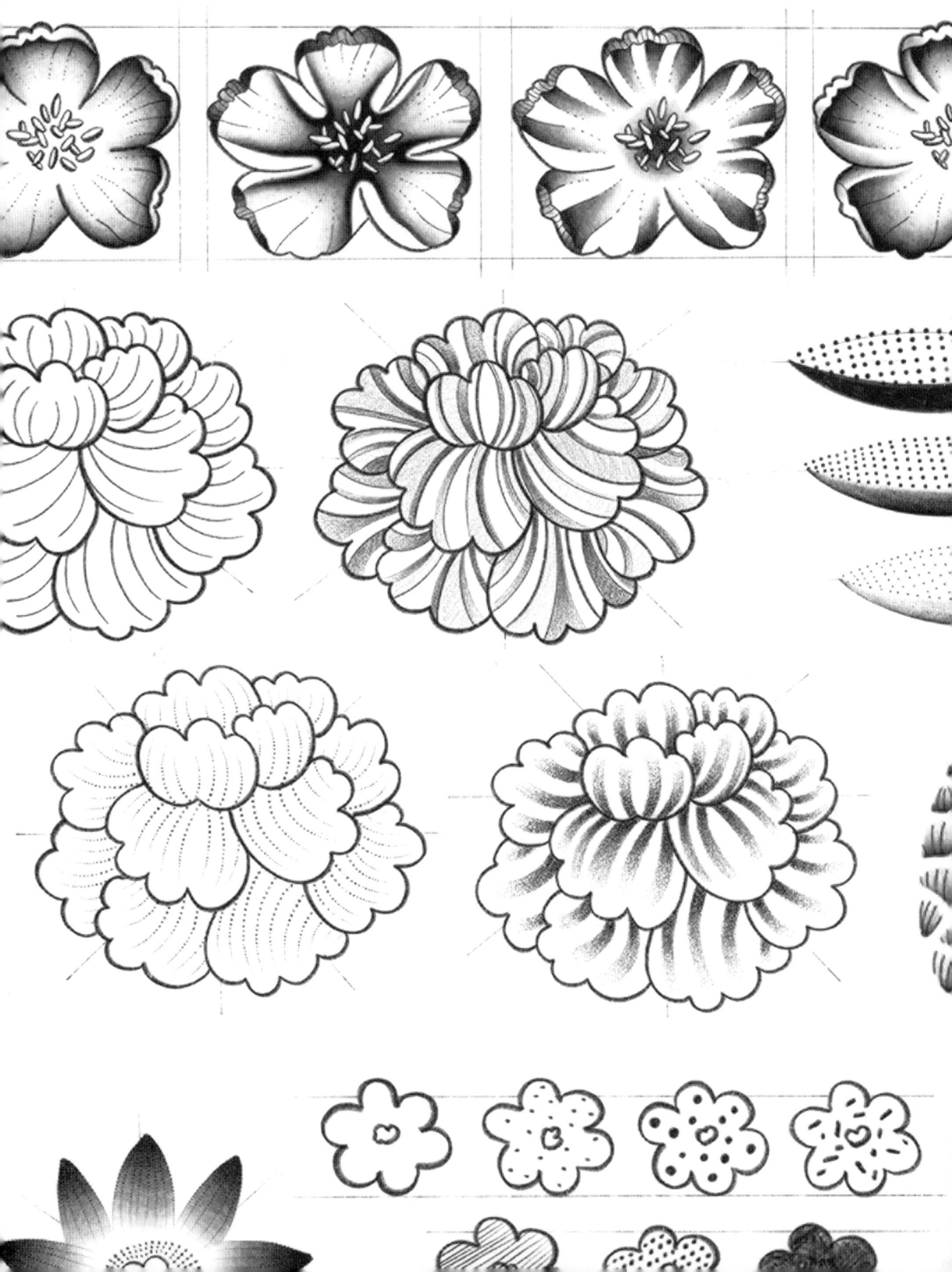

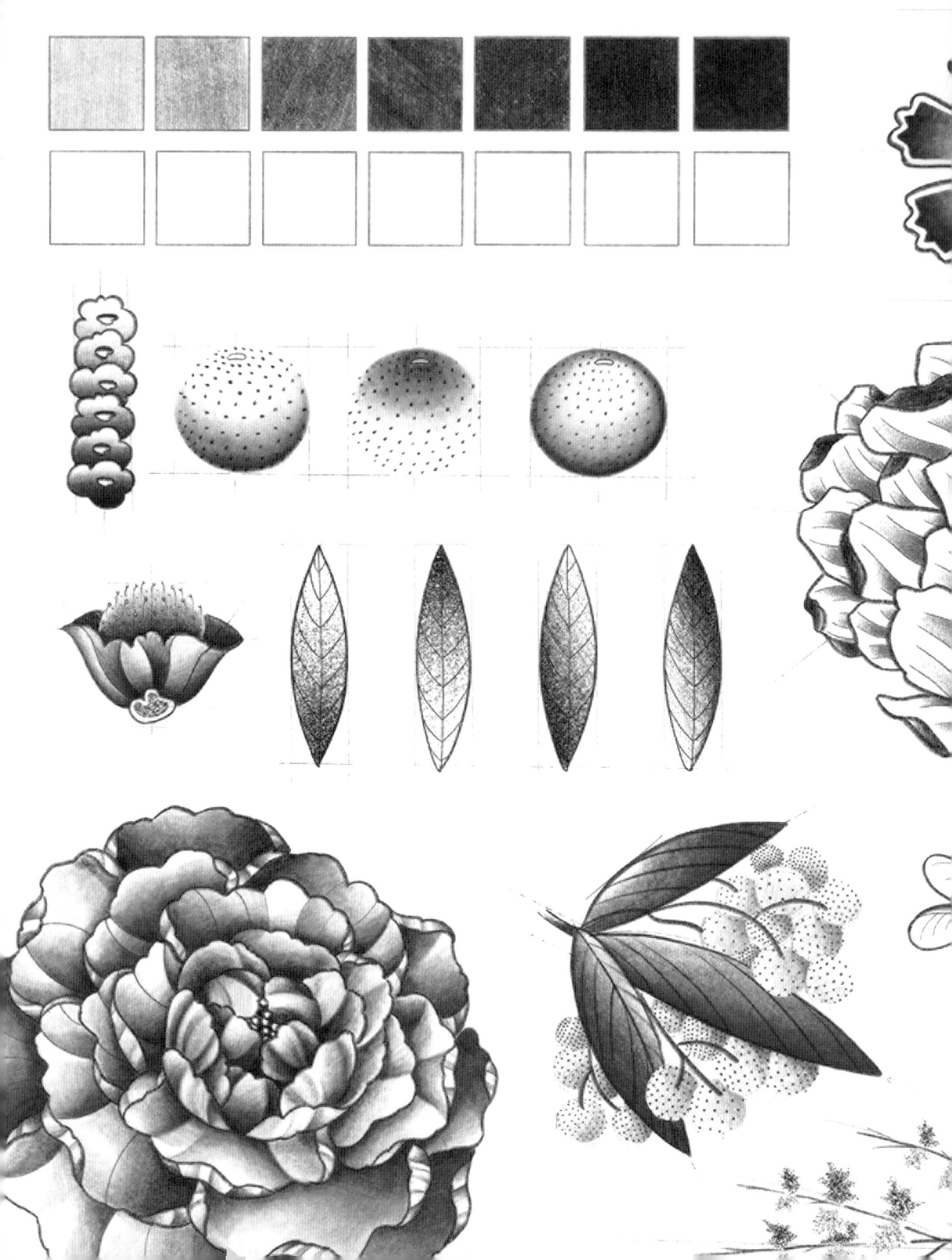

VISUAL STORYTELLING: MIRRORING PLANT CYCLES

Plants are living beings in a constant, steady dialogue with the world around them. They feel the warmth of the sun and turn their leaves to catch its light. Through their root systems, they communicate with each other, warning nearby plants of danger, sharing nutrients and helping one another grow stronger.

So, how can you reflect this awareness in our drawings? If observing a plant in nature, you'll find different stages of growth happening all at once: small buds emerging, full blooms reaching their peak and petals beginning to fade. New leaves sprout while older leaves wilt, all coexisting in a continuous cycle of change.

Many illustrations focus only on flowers in full bloom, but what story does that image really tell? By incorporating different stages of growth, we hint at both the past and the future, giving space for the passage of time to appear in your drawing. Early growth beside a fading bloom reflects the cycle of the plant's life. Bringing multiple stages together can open your drawing to a richer sense of time.

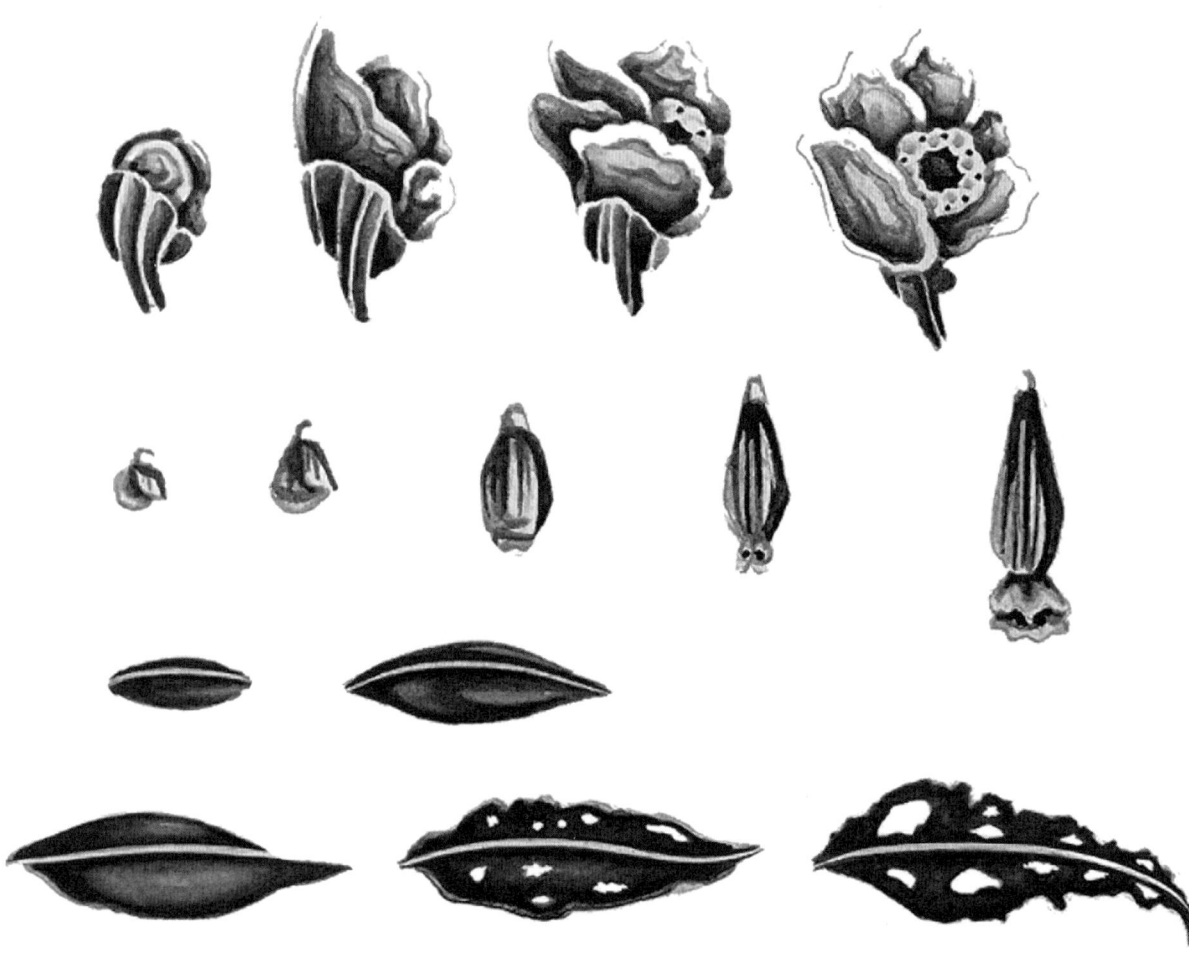

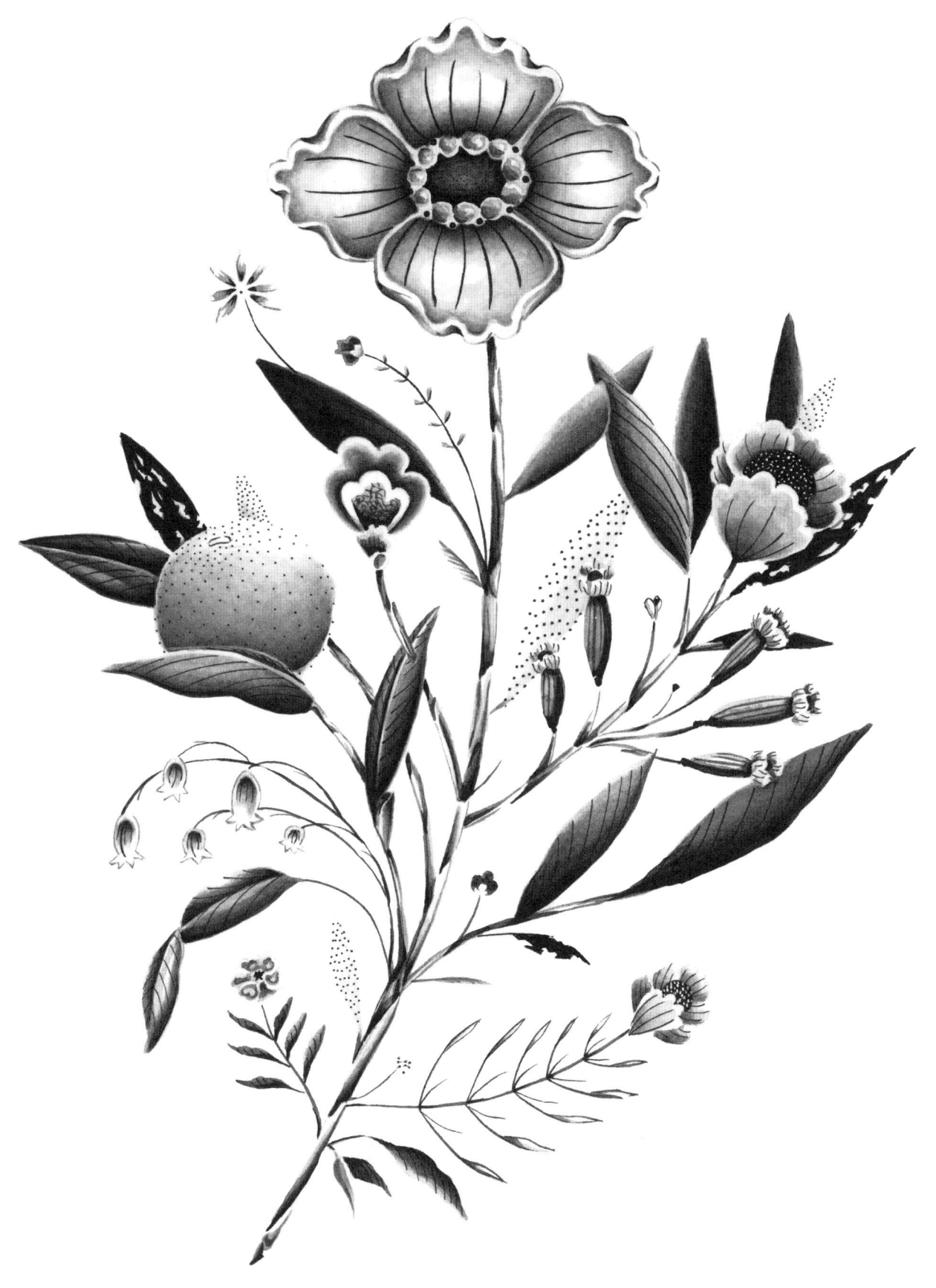

PRACTICE SPACE

Use these pages to explore anything that caught your attention along the way. Sketch plants from different angles, notice negative space, shift your viewpoint, or bring in different stages of growth.

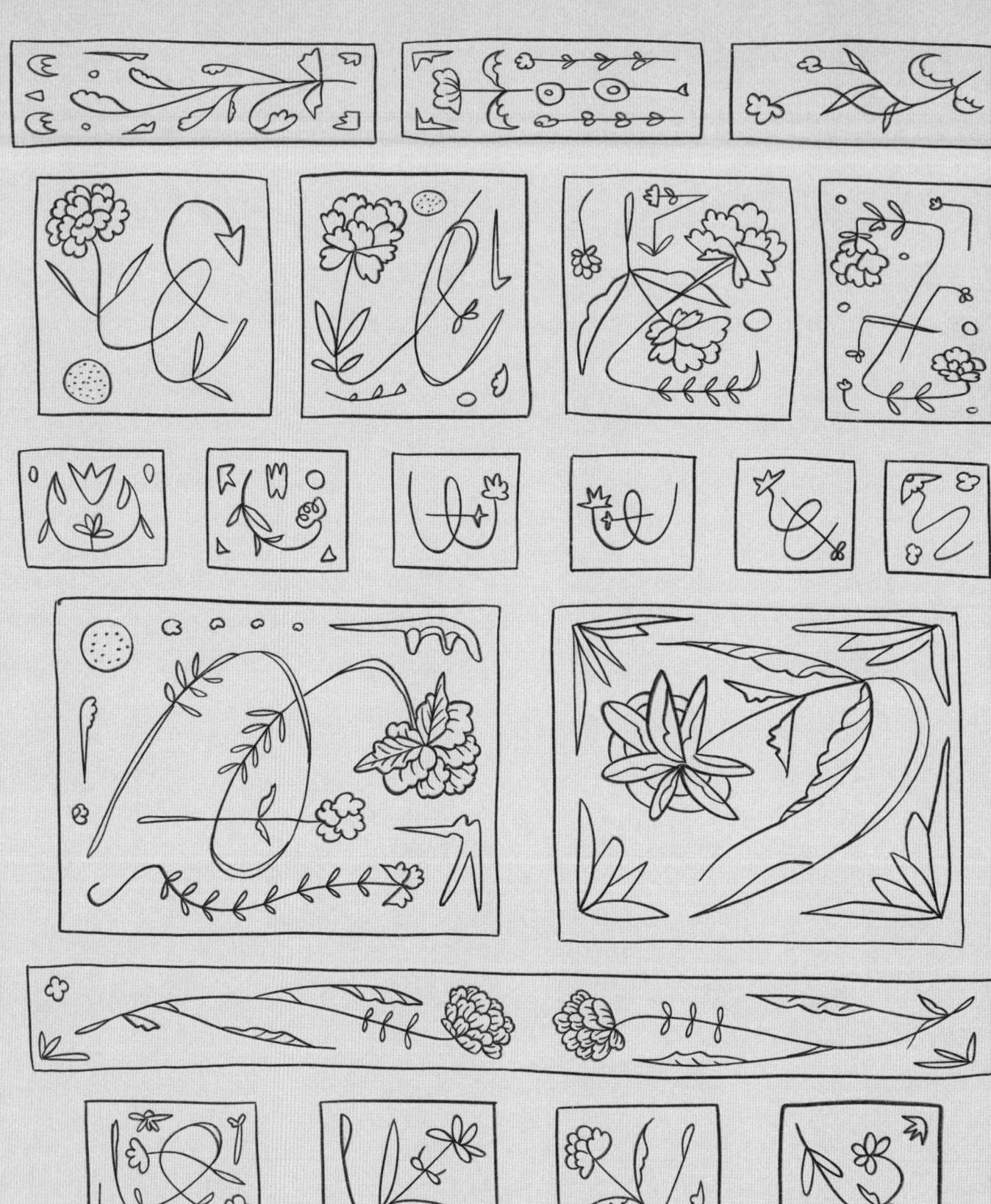

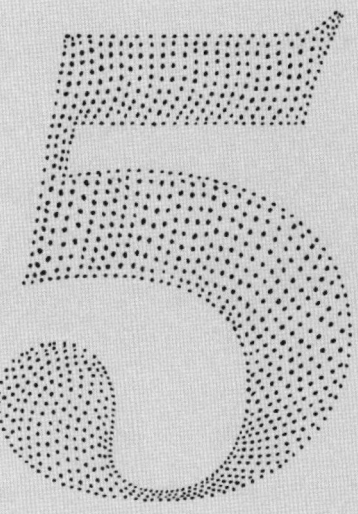

THE BUILDING BLOCKS OF PLANT LIFE

Most botanical illustrations share the essential structures of plant life: stems, leaves and flowers. Together they set the rhythm, balance and character of your drawing.

In this chapter, you'll notice how stems create flow and stability, how leaves generate patterns and movement, and how flowers can bring detail and draw attention. You'll also find practical approaches to working with line, shape and texture, as well as tips and insights gathered through observation.

STEMS AND BRANCHES: MOVEMENT AND FOUNDATION

Stems are the backbone of plants, the closest equivalent to our skeleton. In nature, they carry water and nutrients from the roots to the leaves and flowers. Some stems are strong and rigid, others flexible and delicate. Some creep low across the ground while others stretch upward in search of sunlight.

In your drawing, stems and branches play multiple roles. They provide the structure that holds the composition together, define where leaves and flowers will appear and establish the direction and framework of the page. Their direction, branching and curvature form the pillars of the composition, the base on which everything else will be built. That's why it's essential to understand the direction you want your composition to take from the very beginning.

Just as a tree relies on strong roots to stand tall, your illustration depends on a well-formed stem and branches to give it stability and continuity. Taking time to establish this foundation will shape everything that follows.

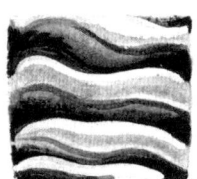 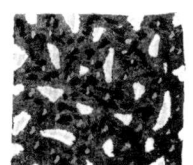 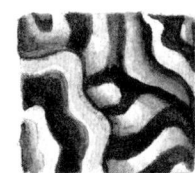 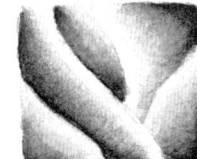 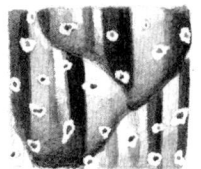

PLAY AROUND

Begin by exploring different shapes and structures; let your instincts guide you. The form and flow of your stem will always evoke a particular feeling, shaping the overall mood and energy of the illustration.

LINE WEIGHT

Line weight changes how a stem feels. It can be a single, fluid stroke or a thicker line paired with a thinner one for depth. Some stems appear bold and solid, others light and delicate. These variations affect the overall balance and presence of the composition.

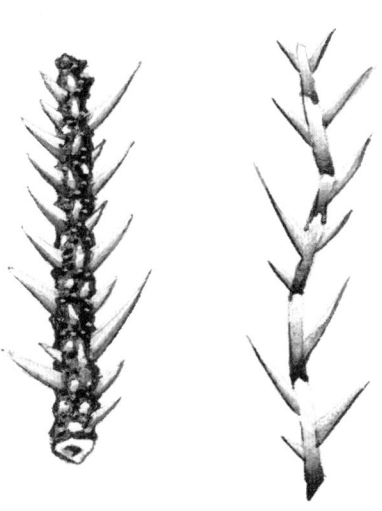
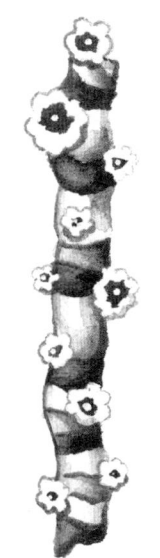
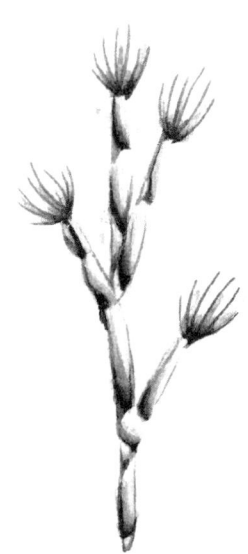
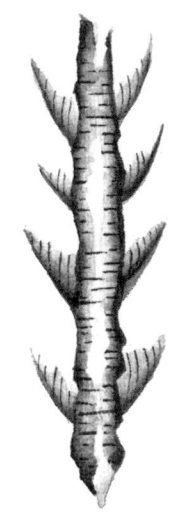

STRUCTURE AND SURFACE

In nature, some stems grow in short, segmented sections while others extend in long, continuous lines. Some carry spikes, others have ridges, grooves or soft textured surfaces. Incorporating these variations into your drawing adds character and presence to the stems, enhancing their contribution to the overall illustration.

NEGATIVE SPACE CHECK

Before adding leaves or flowers, pause to notice the spaces between your stems. These openings matter as much as the lines themselves, influencing the harmony and flow of the composition.

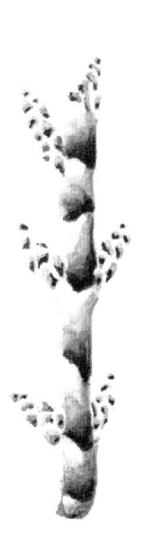
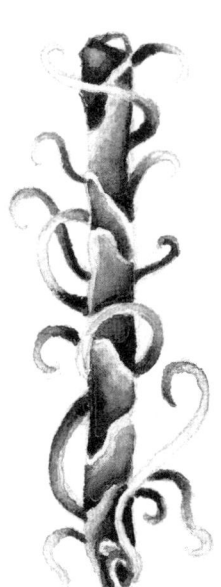
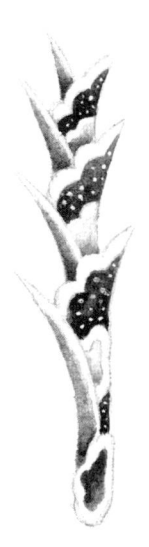
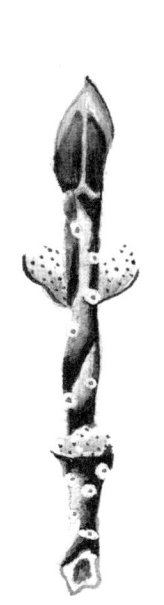
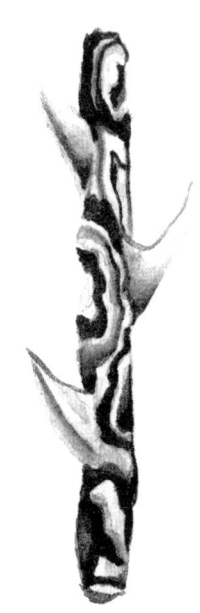

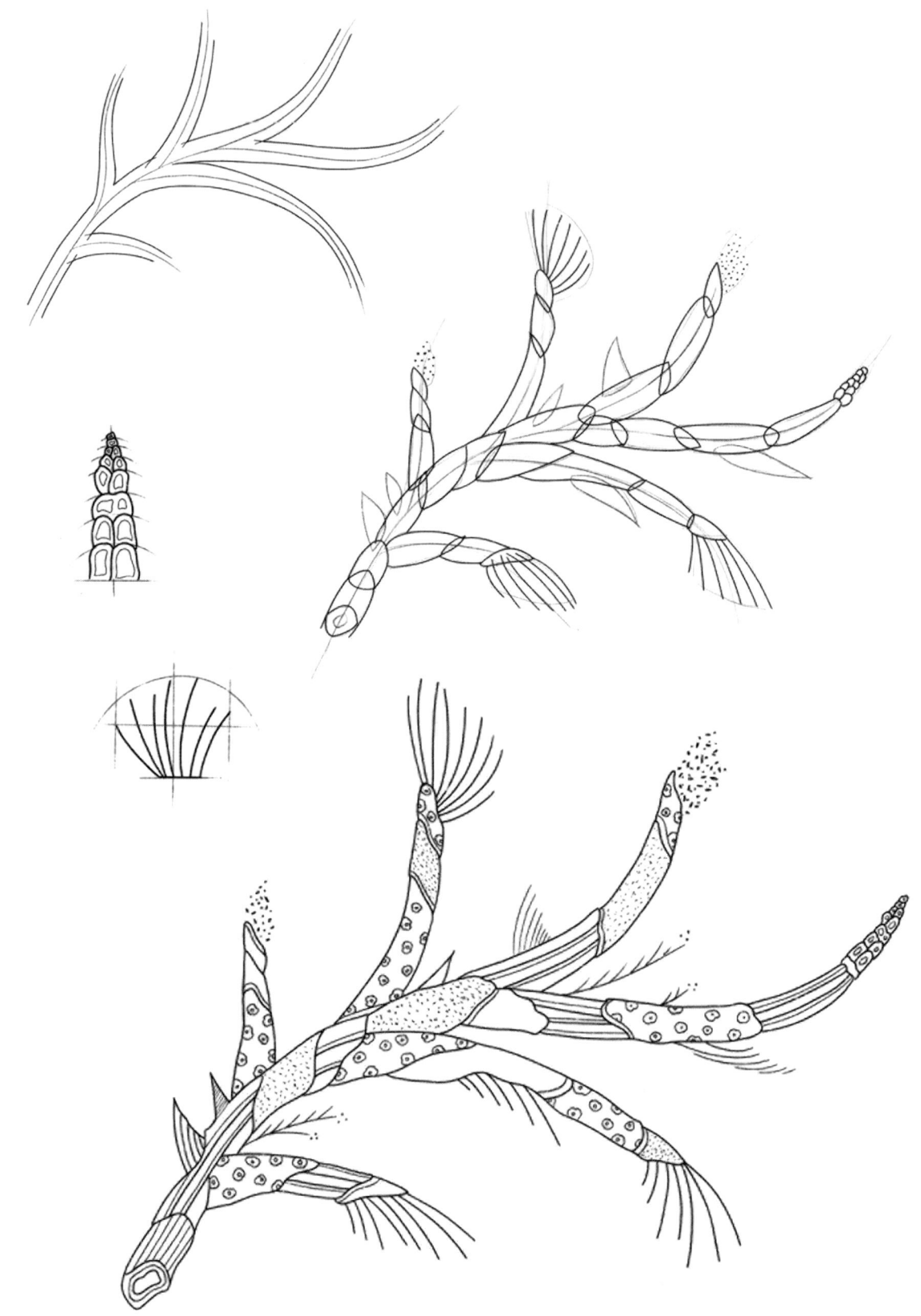

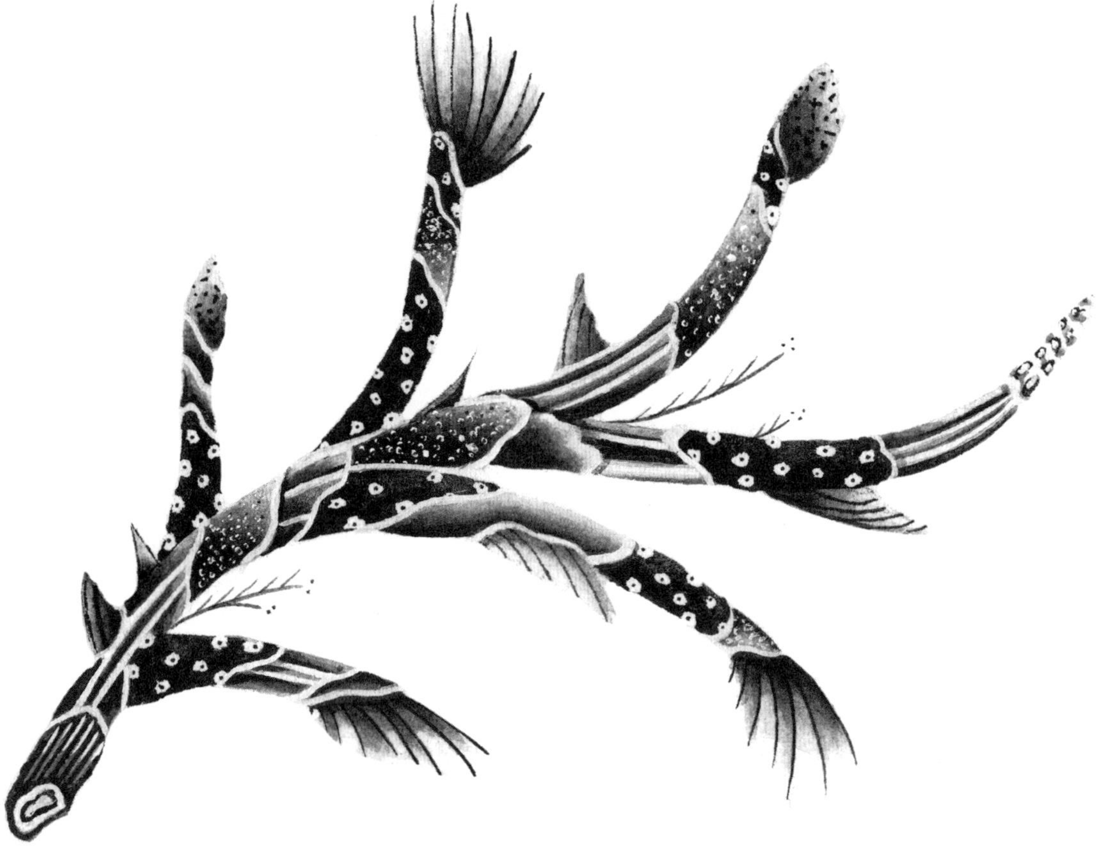

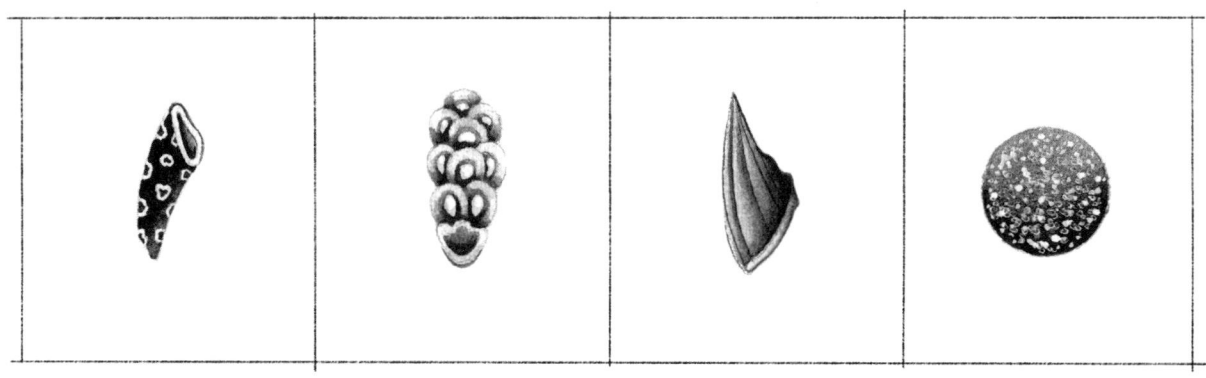

LEAVES: BALANCE AND MOTION

In the plant world, leaves serve many vital functions. They drive photosynthesis, absorbing sunlight and producing the energy that sustains growth. They also come in extraordinary variety, each form reflecting unique adaptations and character.

Leaves are an essential part of your composition, unifying the design and creating movement across the illustration. They weave through the structure, filling spaces, balancing elements and tying the composition together.

If you look closely, you'll see veins running through each leaf, often forming a central line that divides it in two. Many leaves appear symmetrical, with both halves mirroring each other, while others have a more irregular structure, with veins spreading in different directions. These patterns are not only functional but also give leaves their distinct presence – details that help bring cohesion into your drawings.

Because leaves are often the most repeated element in a composition, the way you draw them strongly shapes the overall aesthetic of your illustration.

 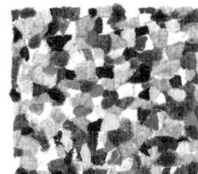 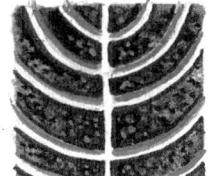 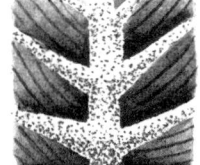 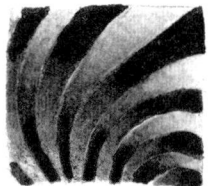

EXPLORING LEAF SHAPES

Each type of leaf brings a distinct character and energy to your illustration. Start by drawing different leaf shapes, focusing on their outlines and noticing how they interact with your composition. Some leaves are broad and rounded, others narrow and pointed, each shape influencing the mood of the piece.

VEINS AND STRUCTURE

There are endless ways to trace veins within a leaf, especially if imagination is your guide. Different vein patterns transform the look of the same silhouette. The placement of the central vein, whether perfectly centred or slightly off, influences the order and movement of the leaf within the composition.

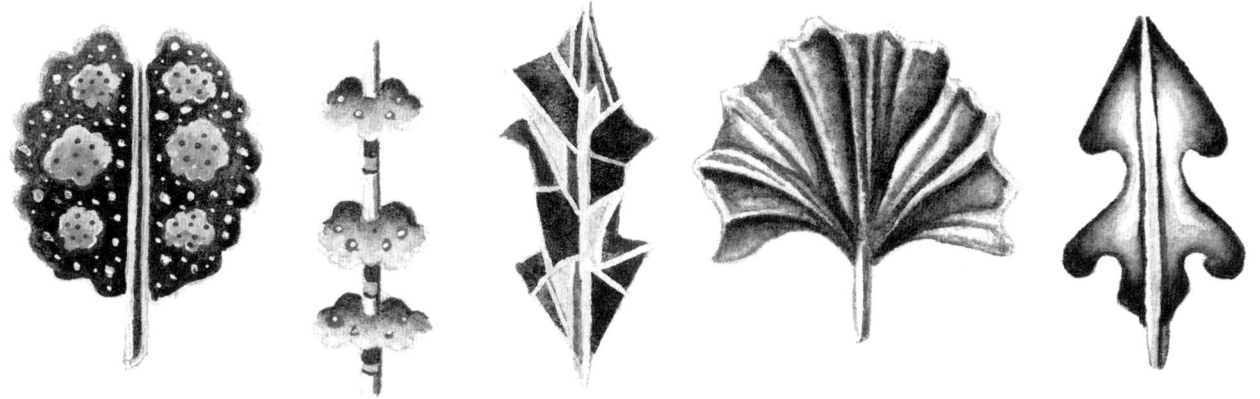

BENDS, TWISTS AND ANGLES

Leaves rarely lie flat; most angle, curl or twist depending on growth and how light interacts with them. Drawing leaves in different orientations introduces a more natural feel. Even a subtle bend or twist can make the leaf appear more dynamic and alive.

EDGES, MARKS AND IMPERFECTIONS

Not all leaves are pristine. Some have smooth edges, others are serrated, wavy or lobed. Some show small tears, curling edges or tiny holes left by insects. Including these details adds character and realism, giving each leaf within the composition a sense of life.

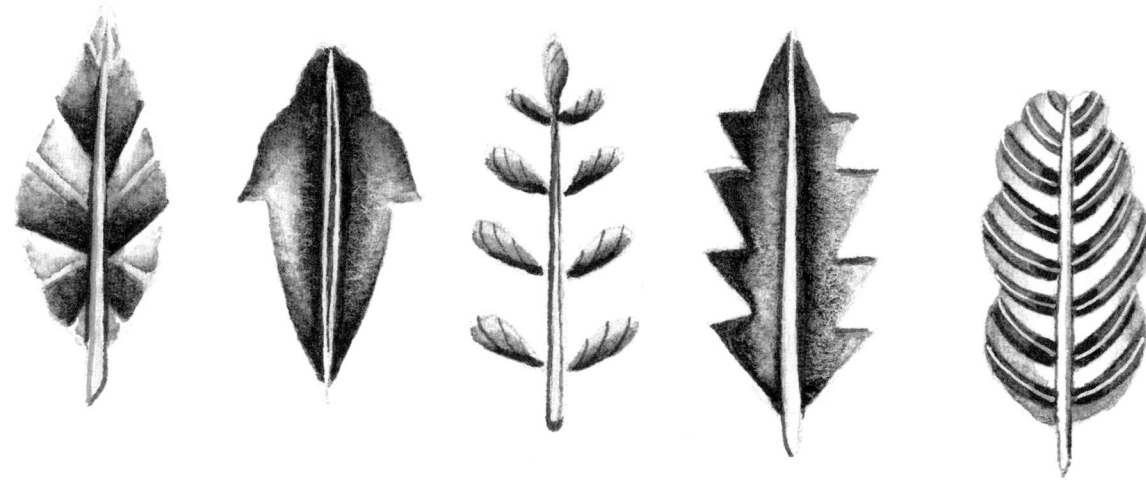

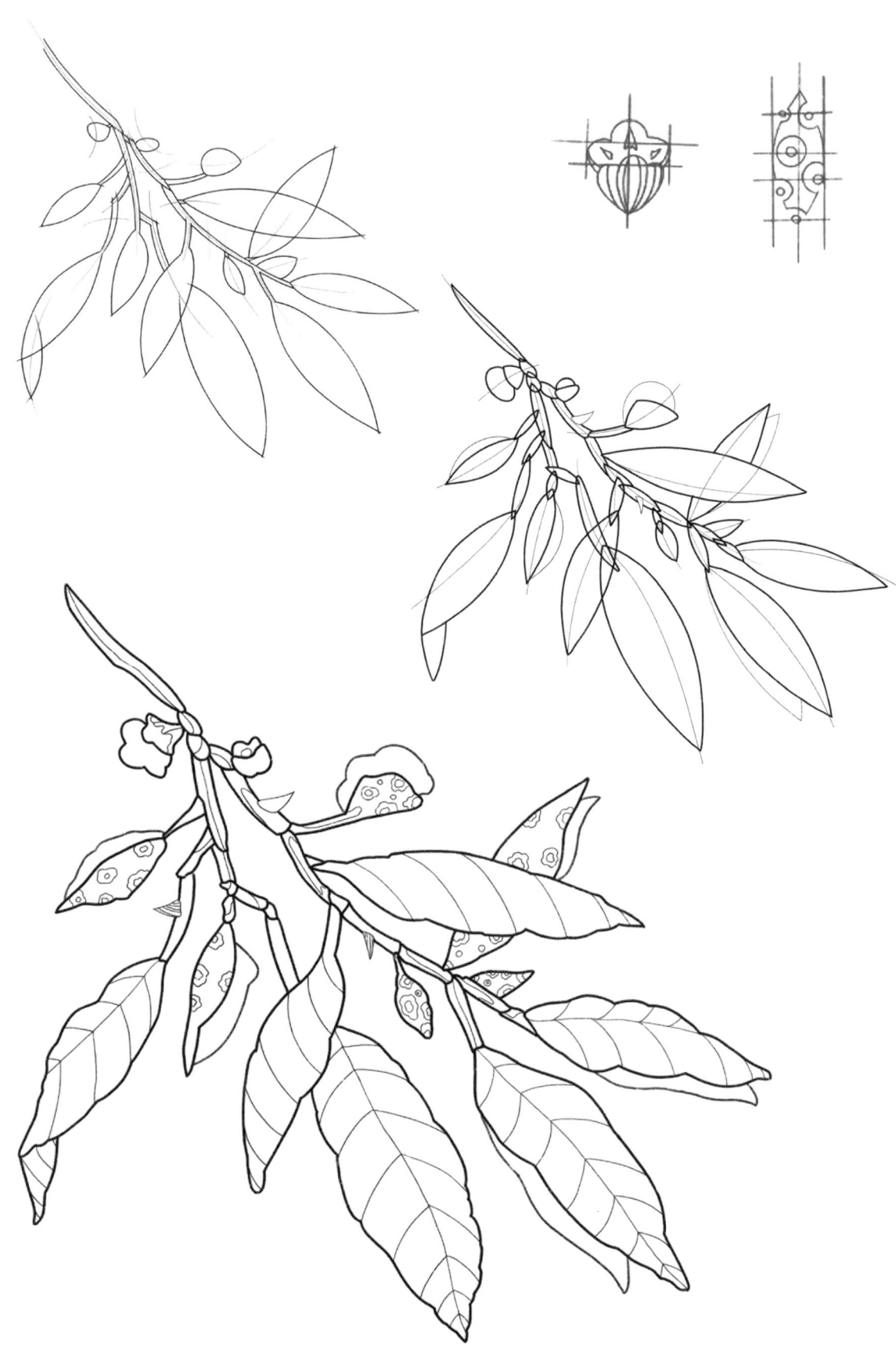

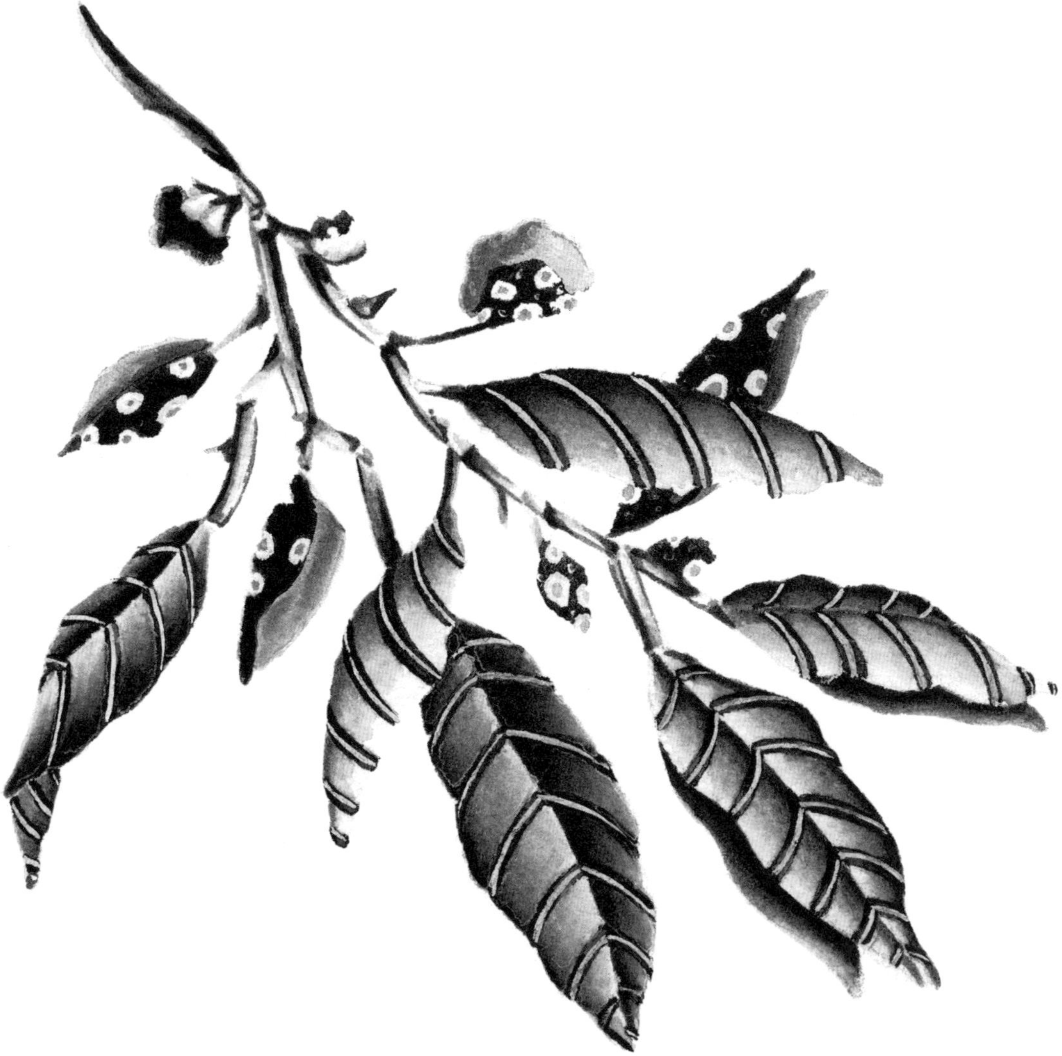

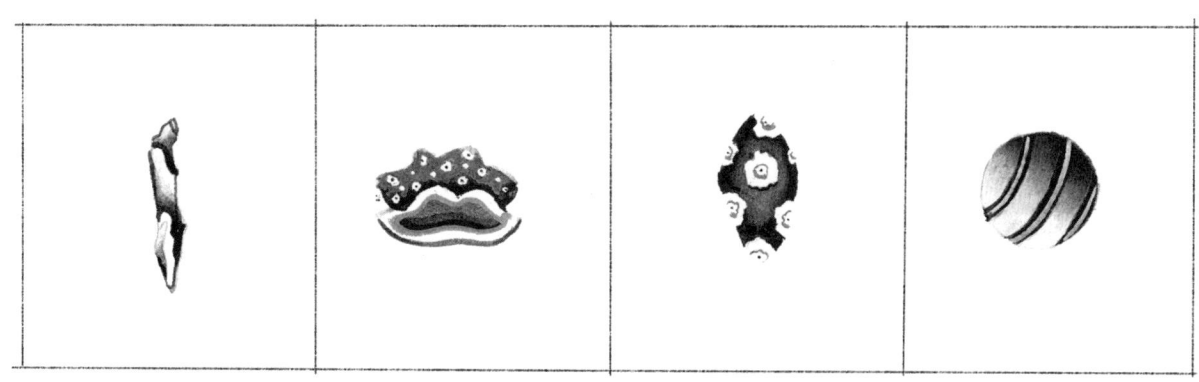

FLOWERS: FORM AND STRUCTURE

Flowers are among the most challenging elements to master, due to the incredible diversity of their shapes and forms. Although these vary widely across species, most follow certain structural patterns, which are important to understand.

In nature flowers play a vital role in reproduction, attracting pollinators with their colours, scent and shapes, while some flowers use wind or self-pollination instead. Some bloom briefly, while others persist much longer, adapting to their environment in fascinating ways. Their forms can be delicate or bold, simple or complex, each adding a different feel and meaning to your drawing.

If you look closely, many blooms share underlying similarities despite their differences – in the way petals are arranged, how buds open or how centres hold reproductive structures. Some forms repeat across species, making it easier to adapt their features, while others are unique.

Recognizing these patterns will help you approach representing flowers with confidence, allowing you to translate their forms naturally into your compositions. In the following pages, I'll guide you through drawing some of my favourite flowers. By understanding their fundamental structures, you'll unlock the ability to draw many other species with ease.

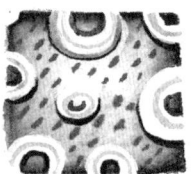 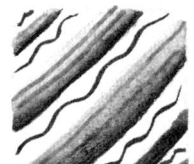 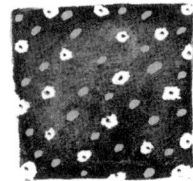 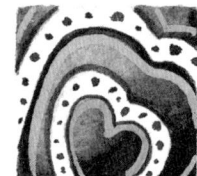 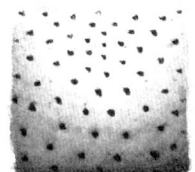

BREAKING DOWN COMPLEXITY

Most blooms can be simplified into basic forms. Start with circles, ovals or soft geometric shapes to establish the overall structure before adding details. This approach makes even the most intricate flowers approachable and helps maintain clarity throughout the process.

PATTERNS AND REPETITION

Many species follow repeating patterns: petals radiating from a centre, overlapping layers or spiralling arrangements. Observing these repetitions in nature provides insight into natural order and helps create more cohesive floral illustrations.

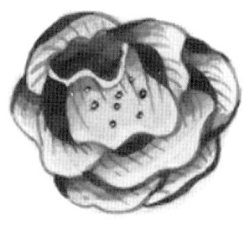  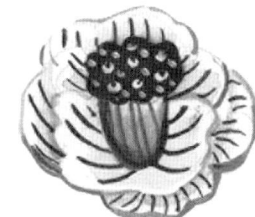 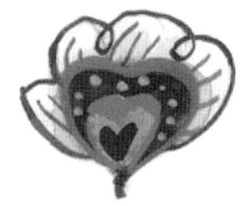 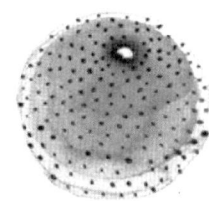

PETAL INTERPLAY

Petals can overlap, tuck behind one another or turn at different angles. These shifts are often simpler than they first appear, and by observing them you can see how each petal connects to the next.

PERSPECTIVE AND MOVEMENT

Flowers rarely face straight ahead. They tilt, fold or curve, altering their shape depending on the viewing angle. Practising these variations adds richness and variety, while a slightly turned or partially closed bloom can create a sense of contained movement within your composition.

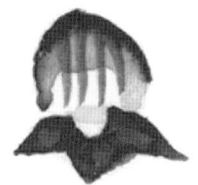 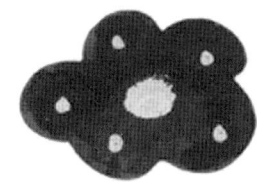 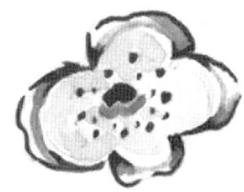 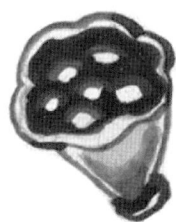 

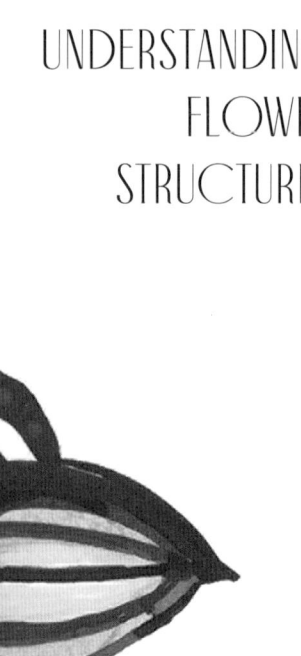

UNDERSTANDING FLOWER STRUCTURES

The universe reveals itself through recurring patterns - in the steady paths of stars across the sky, the lines pressed into sand by the sea or the spirals that shape a pinecone. Flowers are no exception.

Their petals twist, curl and cluster as they bloom, repeating structures that appear again and again across species, shaped by the same rhythms that govern the rest of the natural world.

At first, the details of a flower can feel overwhelming. With practice, patterns begin to emerge. You stop chasing every petal and start to see the flower as a whole rather than getting lost in its complexity. Recognizing this shift makes it easier to approach new species with clarity and confidence.

Whenever possible, spend time with real flowers. Notice how petals unfold, touch their textures, and follow the changes as they bloom or wilt. This kind of looking sharpens your eye and helps you develop sensitivity to their structure.

On the following pages you'll explore four fundamental groups: trumpet-shaped, radial, multi-petal and clustered. They are presented as imaginary flowers, so you can pay attention to their structure rather than specific species. Studying these groups will build your confidence to approach countless real flowers. Once you're familiar with them, you can begin to experiment – changing petal shapes, trying different shading patterns and observing how each choice shifts the result.

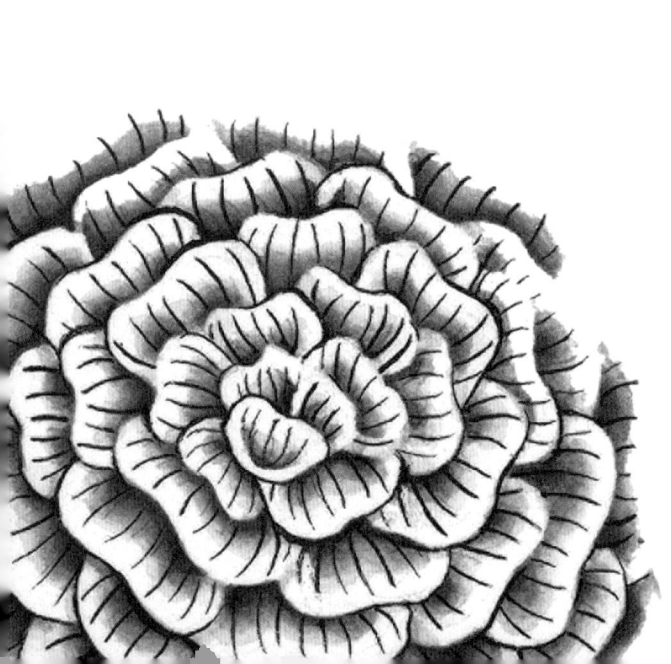

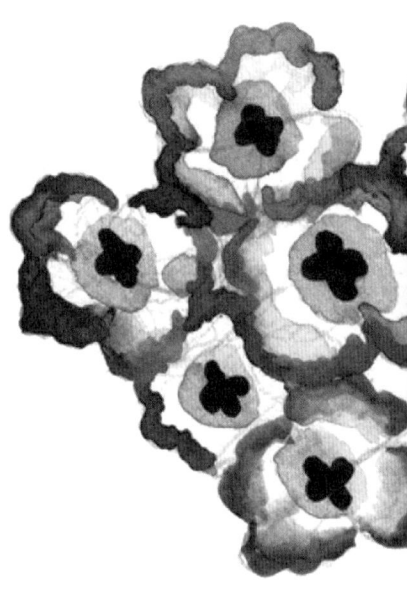

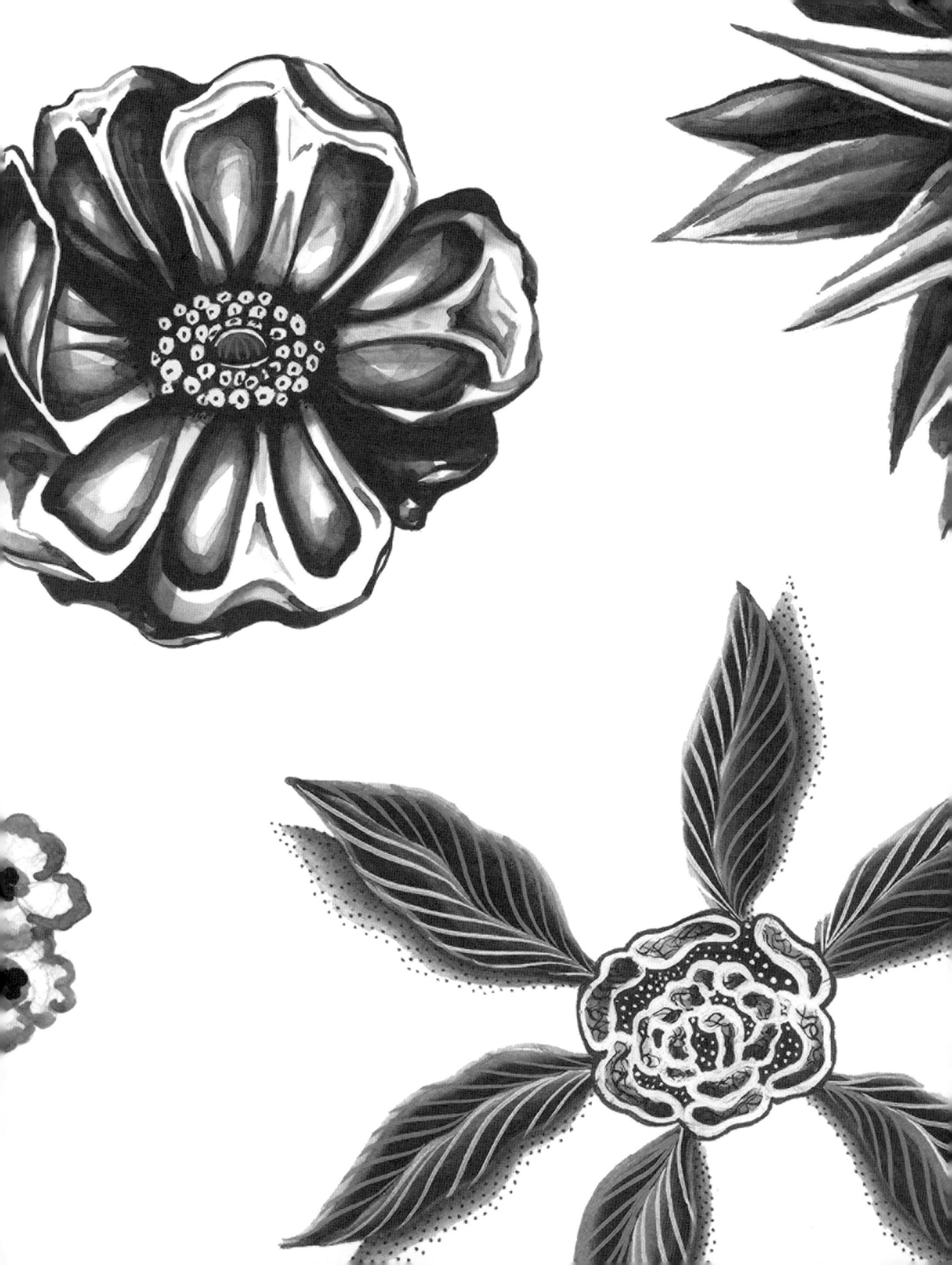

TRUMPET-SHAPED FLOWERS
(e.g., Daffodil, Lily, Morning Glory)

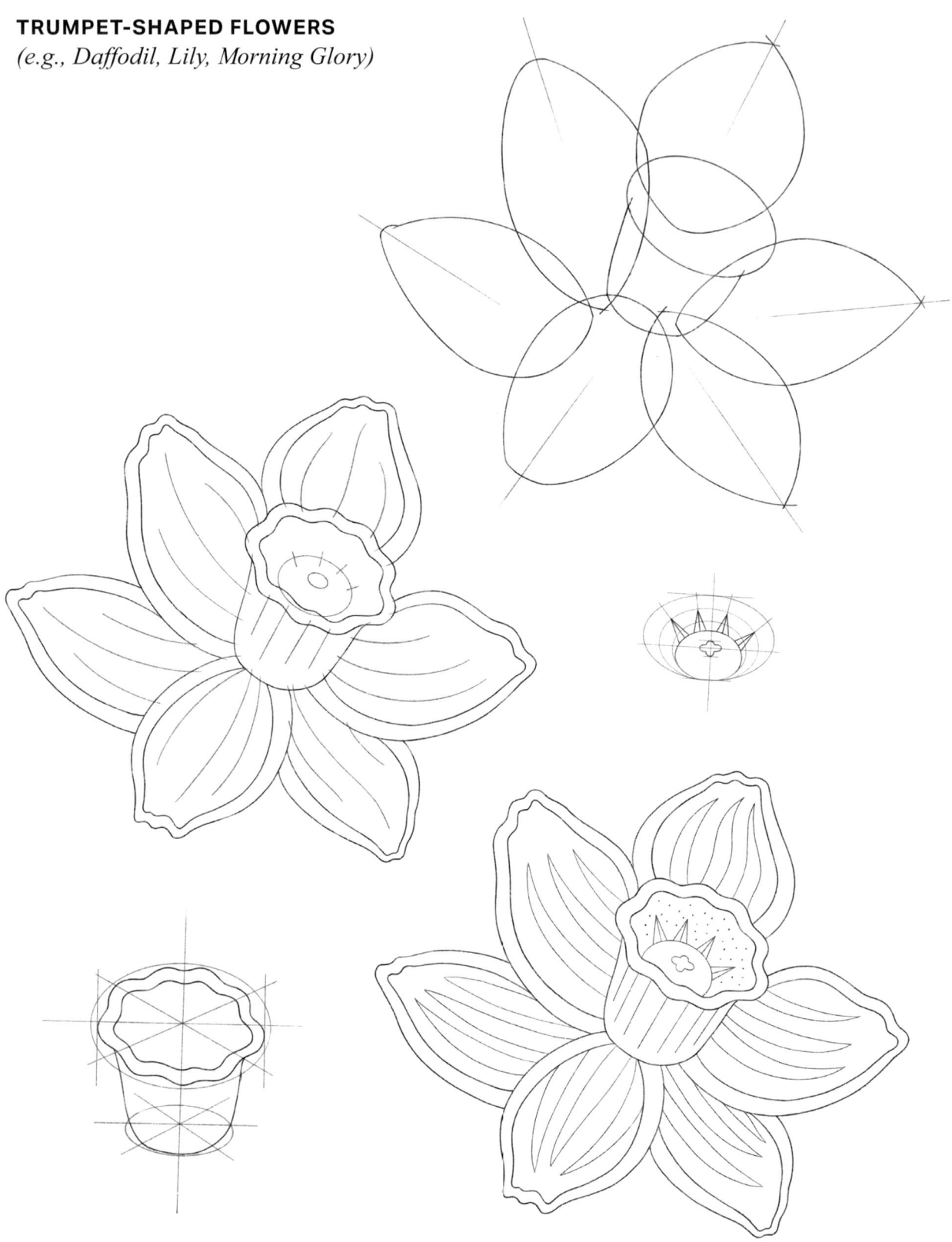

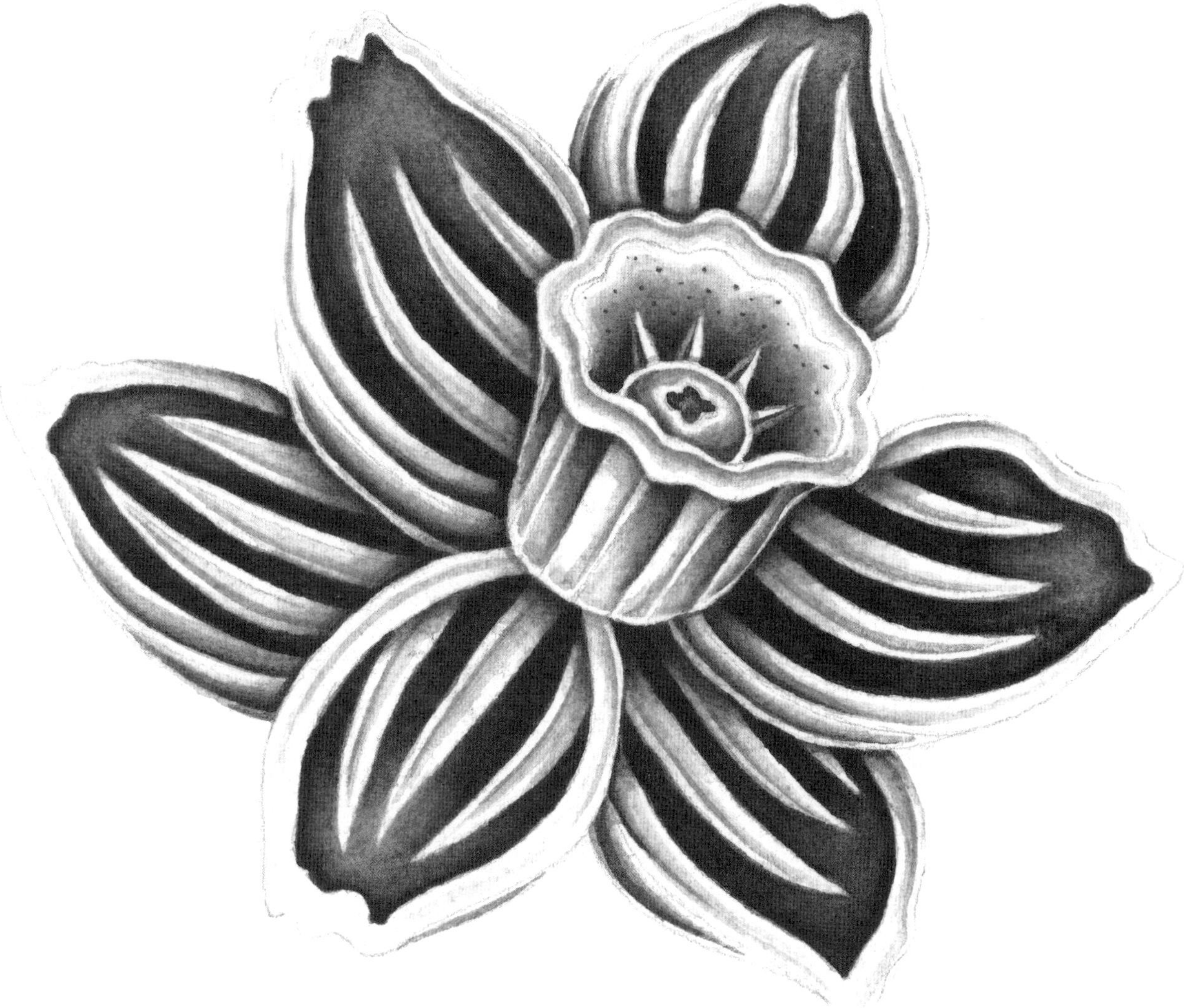

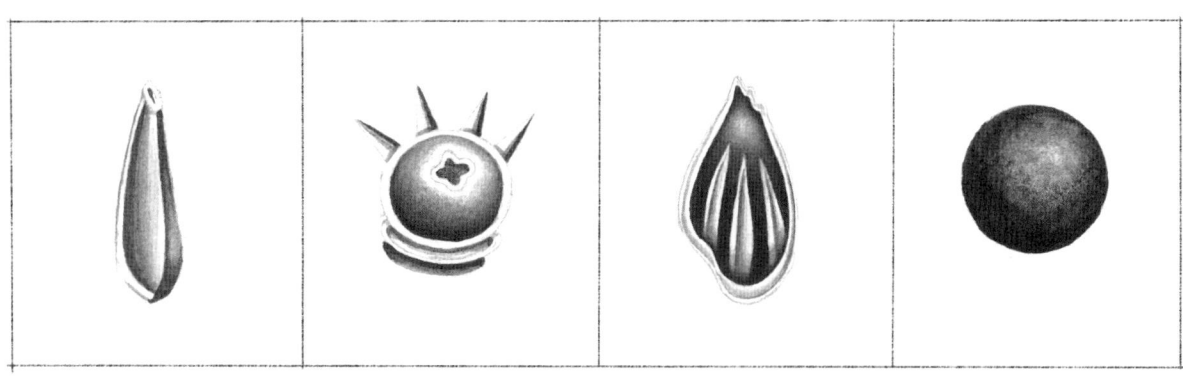

FLAT, RADIAL FLOWERS
(e.g., Anemone, Daisy, Sunflower)

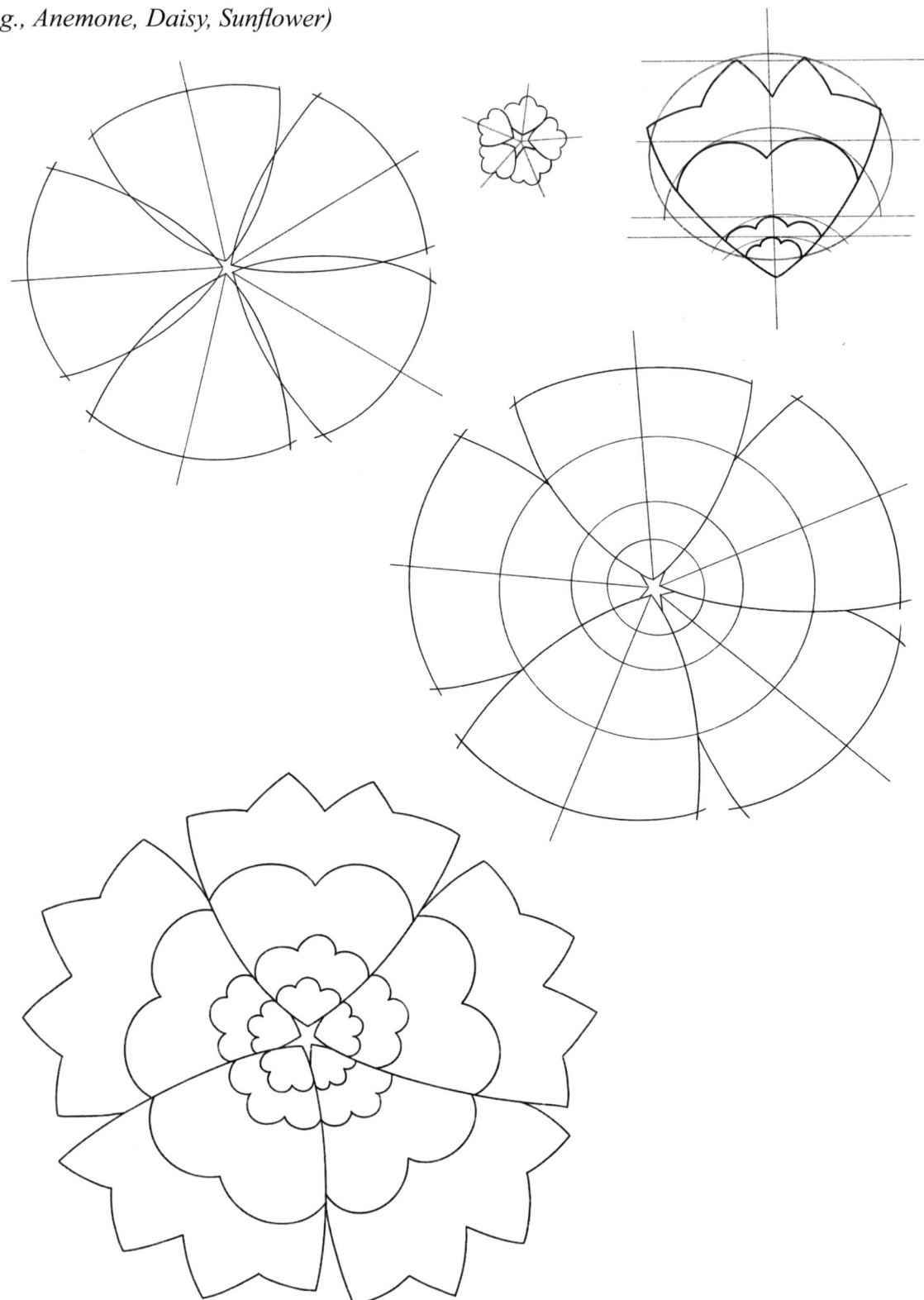

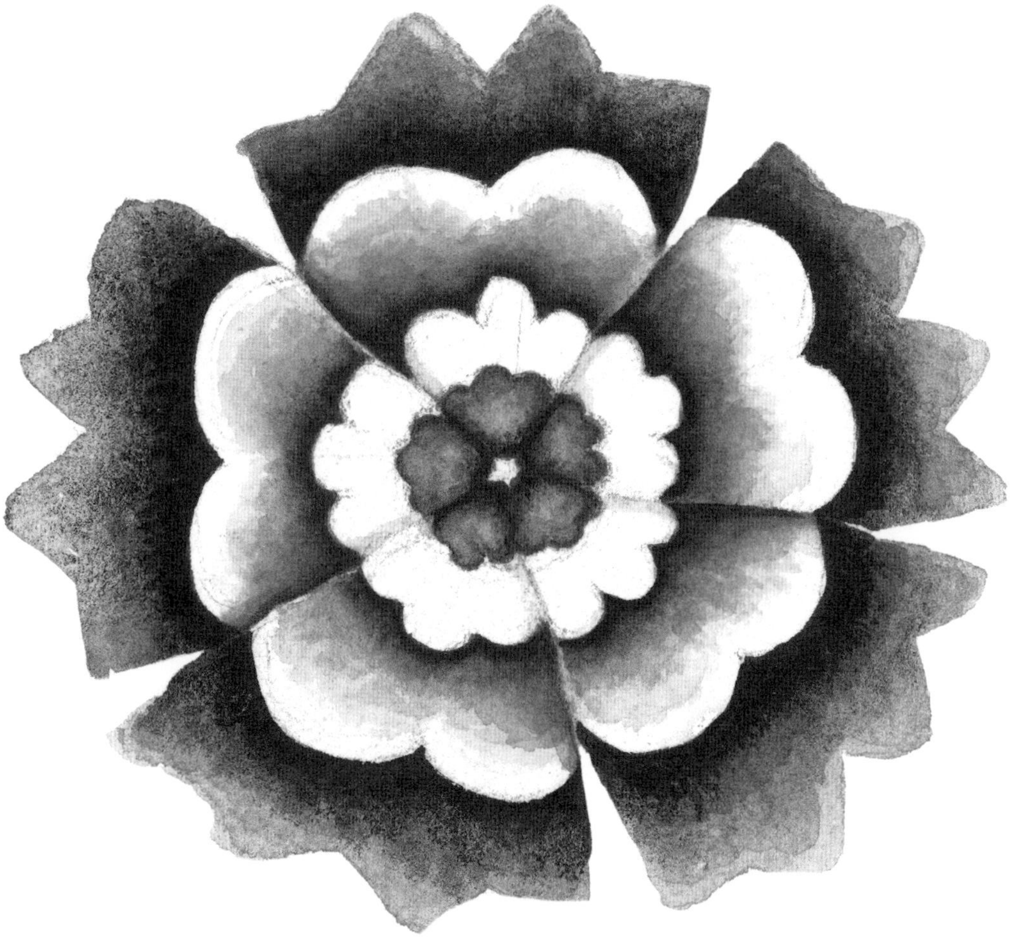

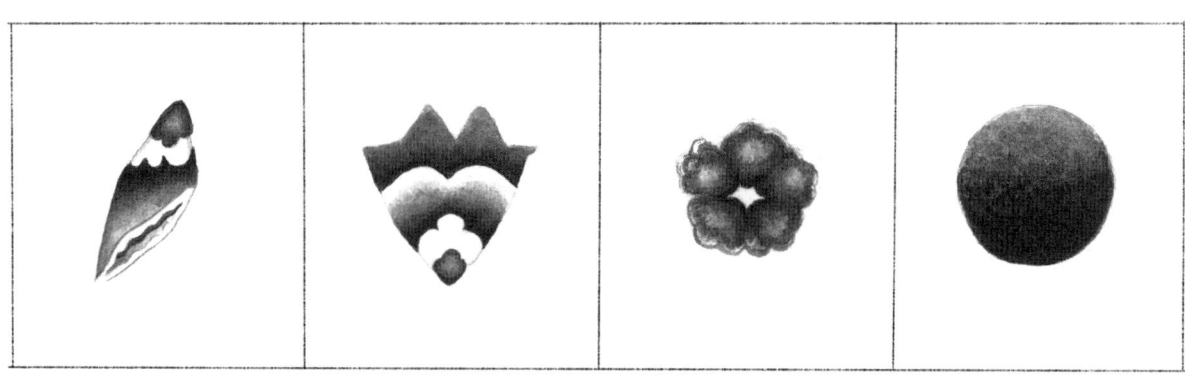

MULTI-PETAL FLOWERS
(e.g., Dahlia, Peony, Zinnia)

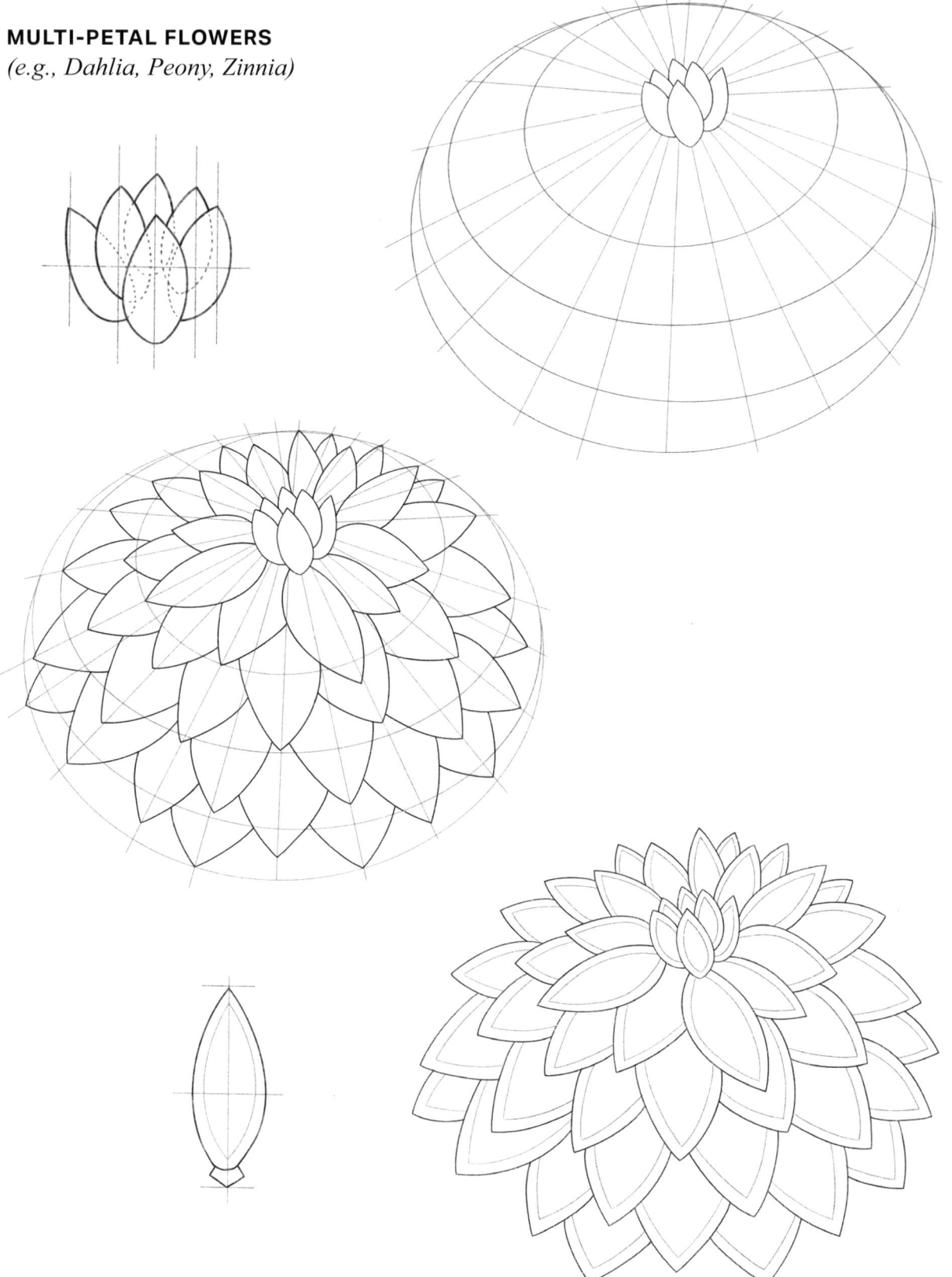

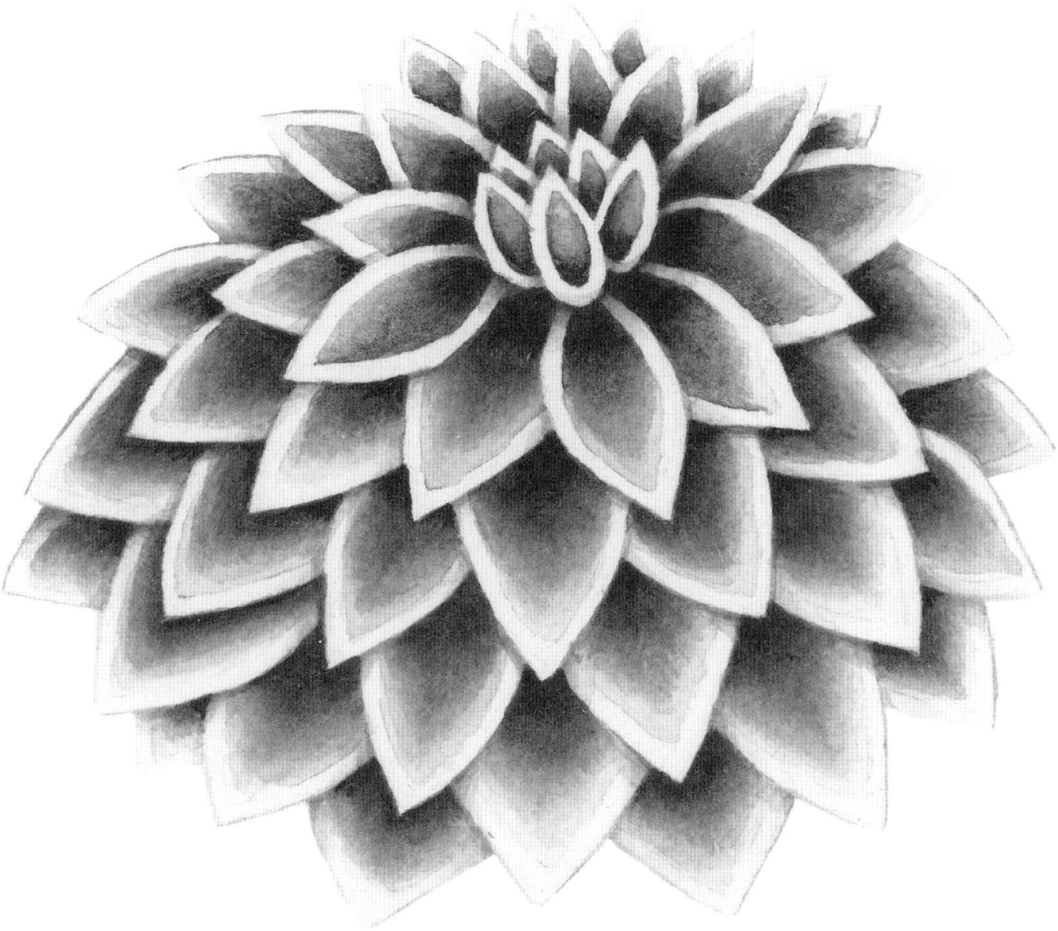

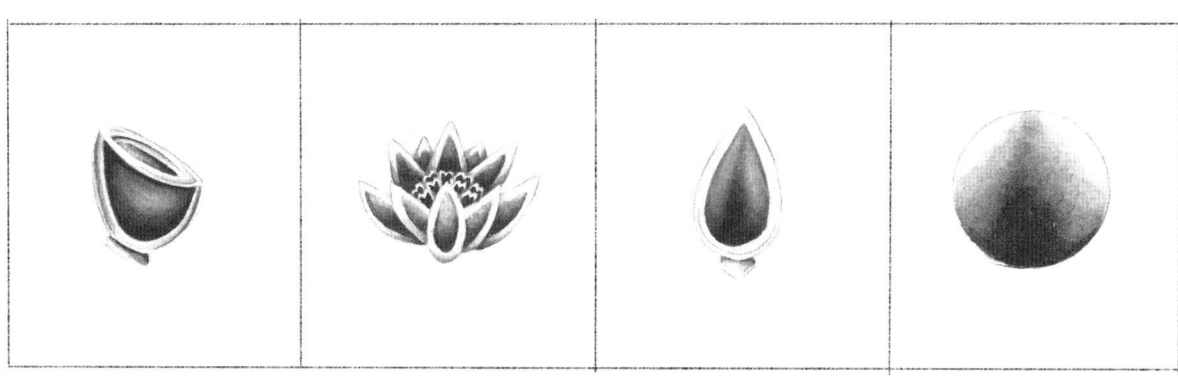

CLUSTERED FLOWERS
(e.g., Hydrangea, Lilac, Wisteria)

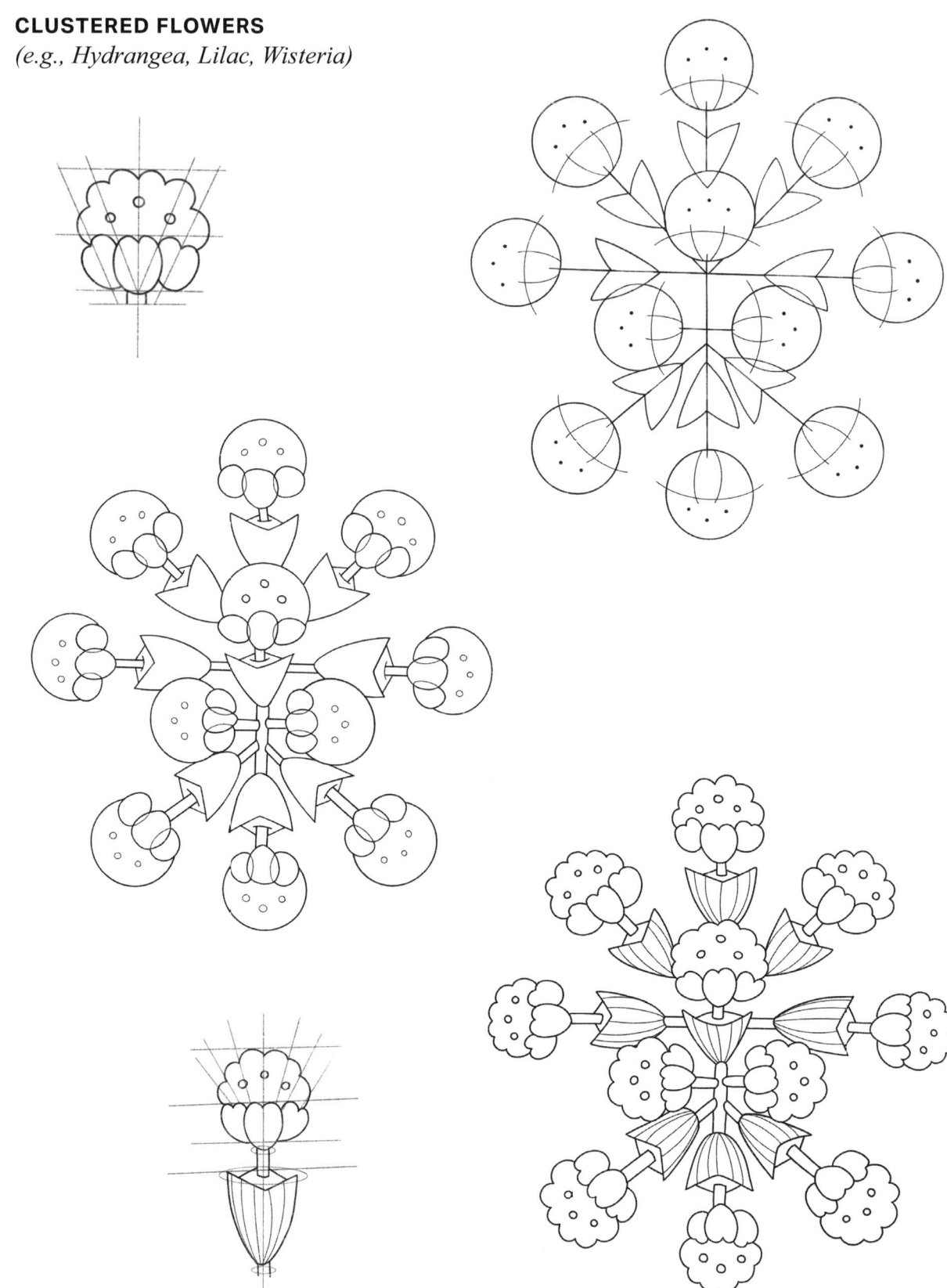

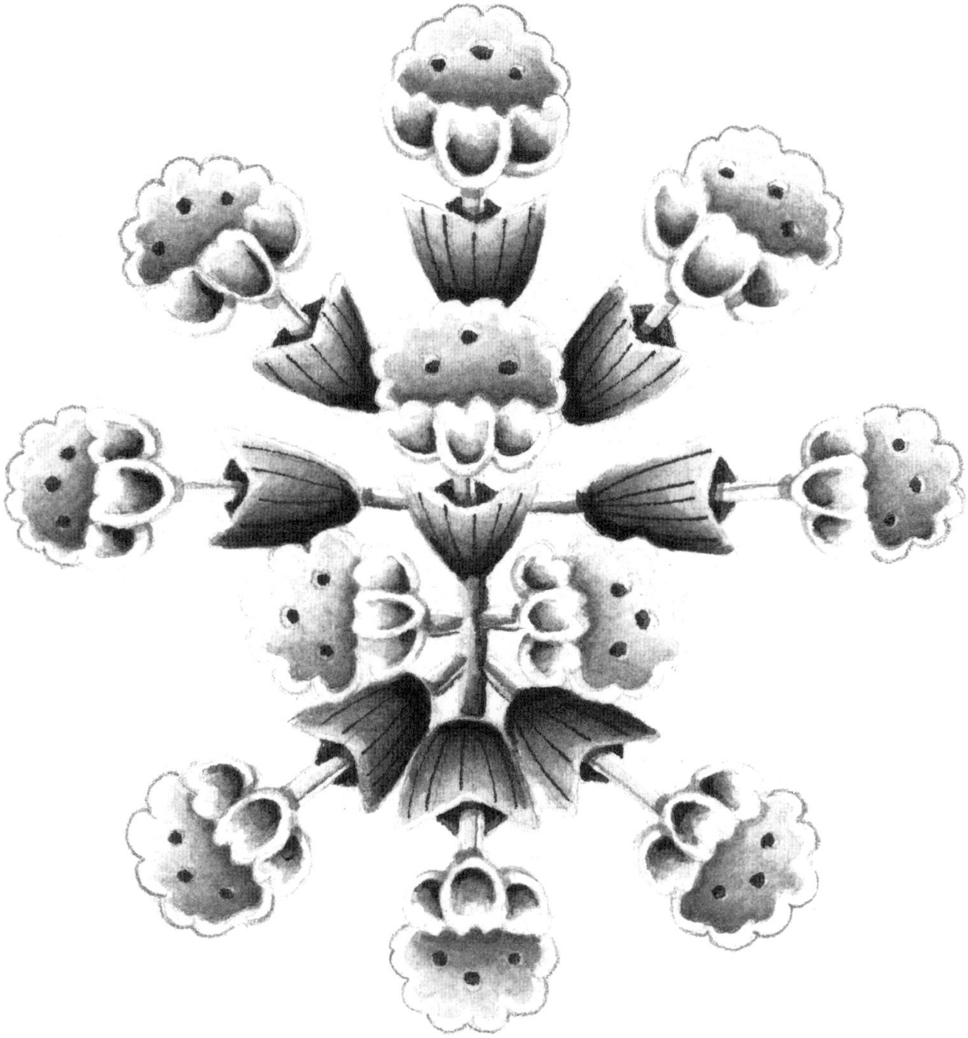

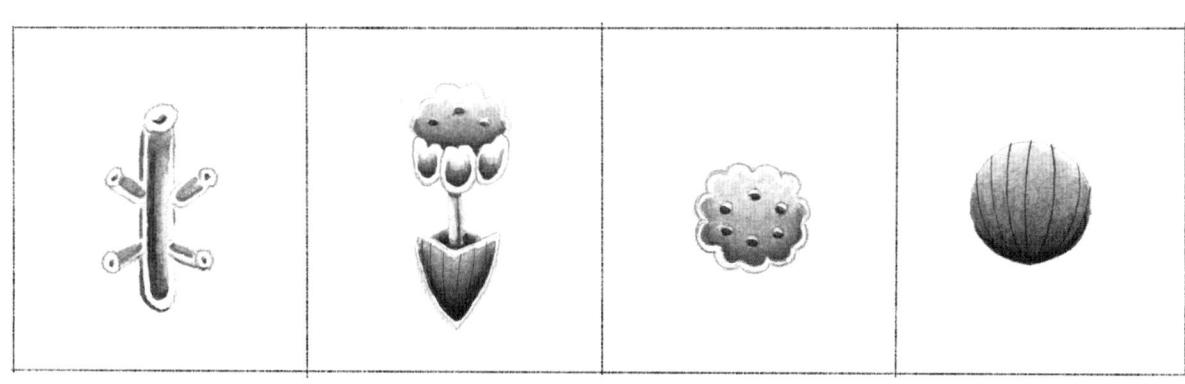

FORM STUDIES

Let this spread collect whatever you'd like to try from this chapter. You can play around with different stem directions, leaf shapes, or explore how each flower structure might translate into other blooms.

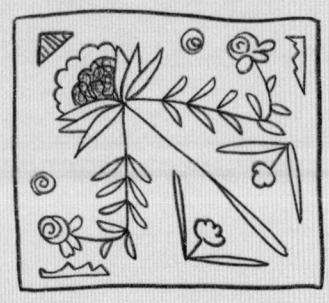
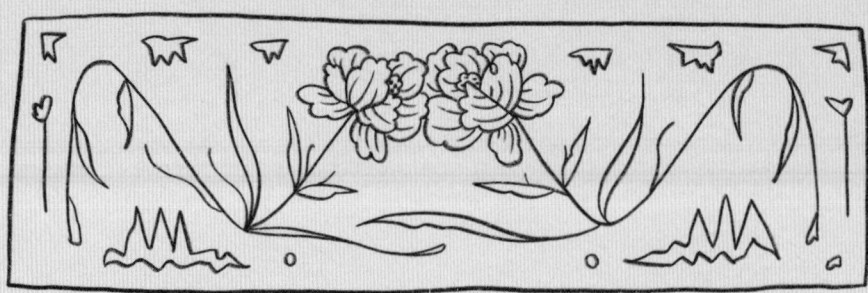
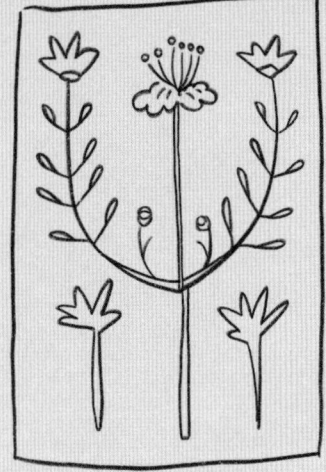
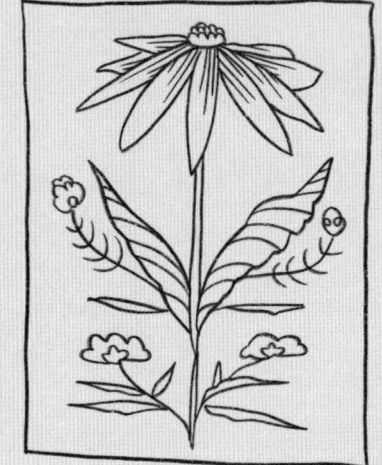
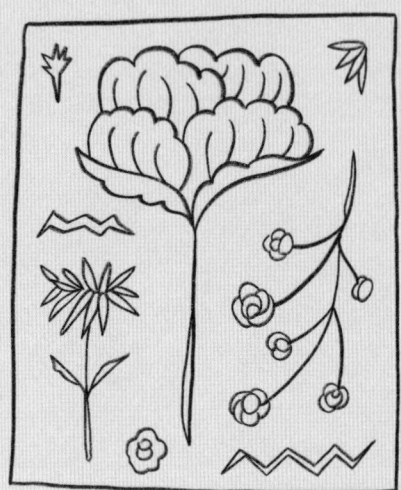
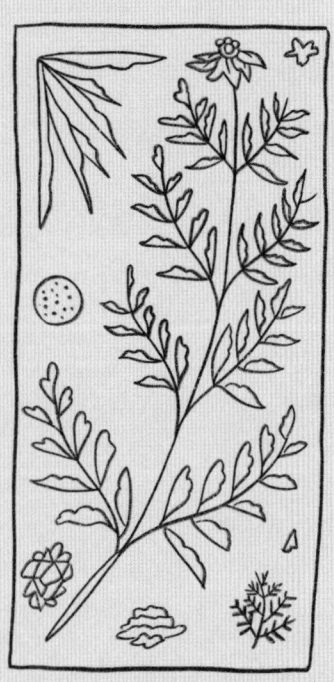
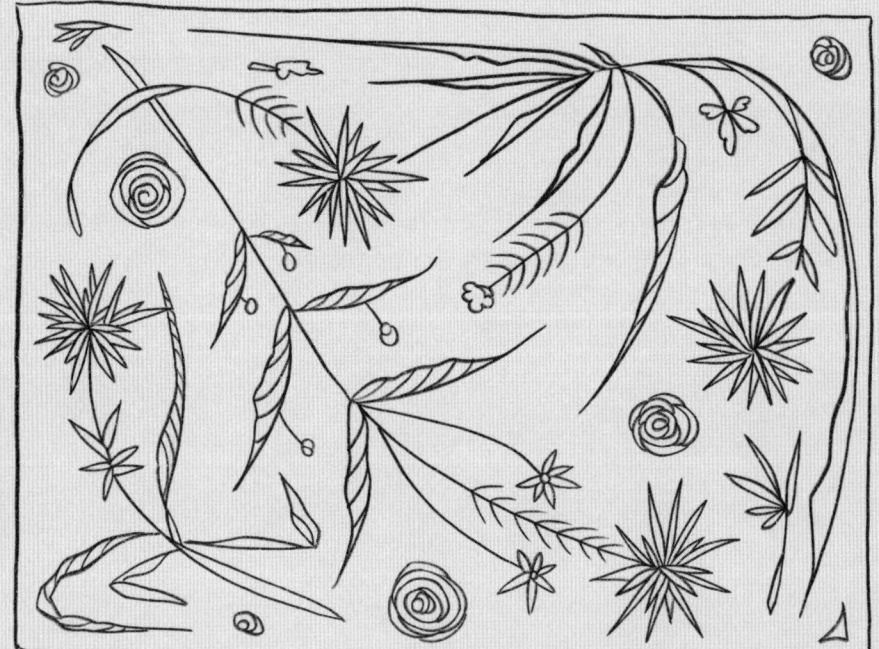
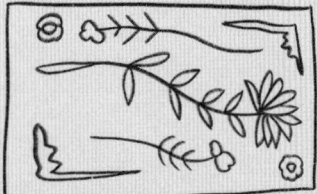

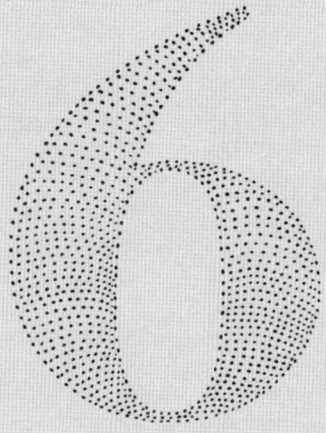

FLOWER ARRANGEMENT

There are endless possibilities when combining botanical elements on a page, yet what matters most is working toward compositions that feel intentional and alive.

A strong composition carries rhythm that sparks curiosity and draws the viewer into your world. In this chapter, you'll consider movement, balance and depth, discovering how small choices can shift the character of a whole arrangement.

The pages ahead are an invitation to experiment, to see how each decision - whether about mood, rhythm or detail - gradually comes together as a drawing that has a life of its own. Having practised stems, leaves and flowers separately, now is the time to bring them together, shaped by how you feel and experience the plants around you.

CREATING FLOWER ARRANGEMENT

Once you let go of representing plants exactly as they appear in nature, the possibilities are endless, opening a world where any plant can be combined with another, even those that would never have crossed paths in the wild.

To create a composition that feels organic and alive, it's important to let the elements intertwine and respond to one another, creating a sense of unity and belonging.

The next pages offer a starting point, and with time and consistent practice your arrangements will soon take on a life of their own. Feel free to use the sketches provided to begin with, or draw your own.

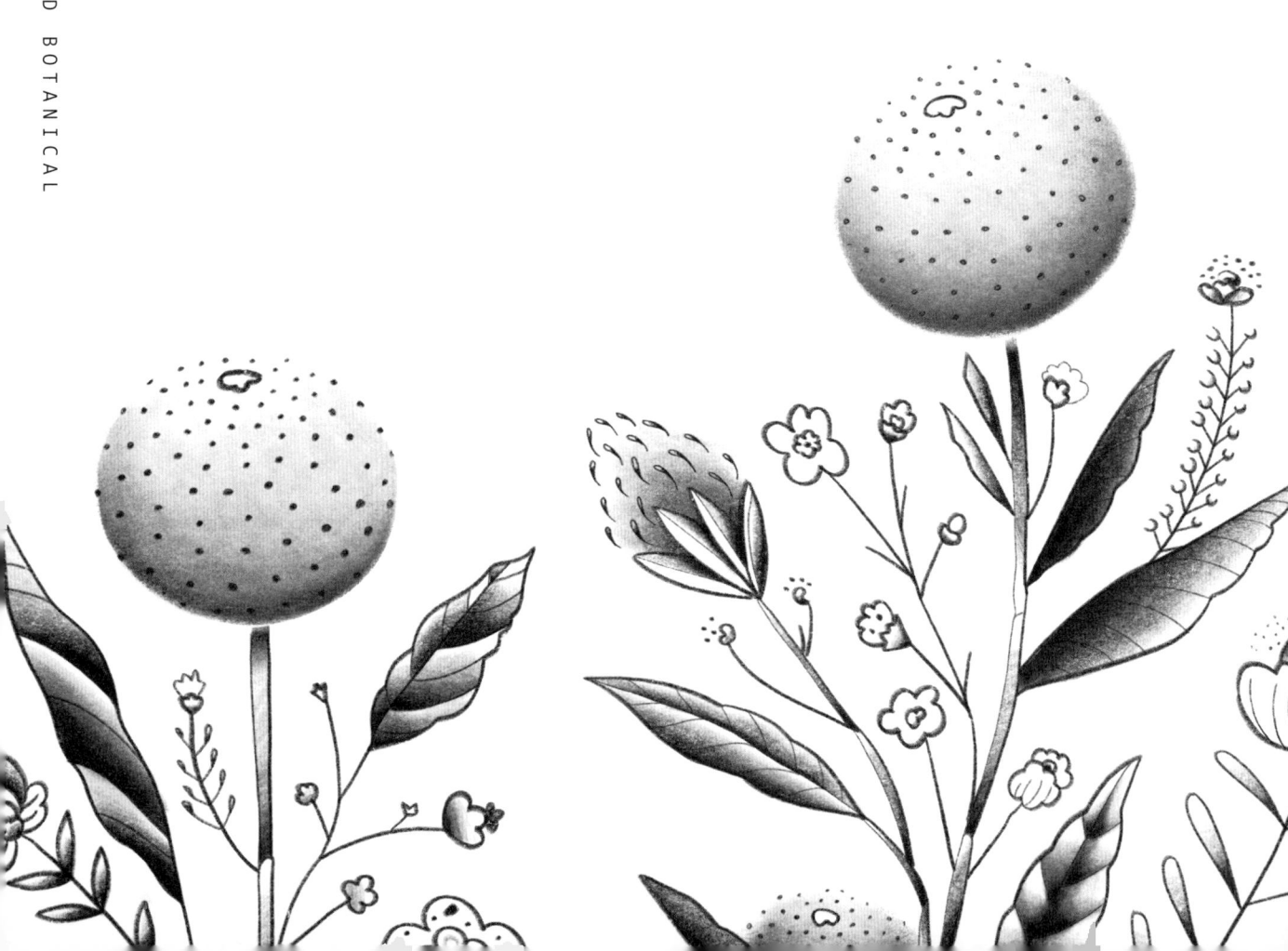

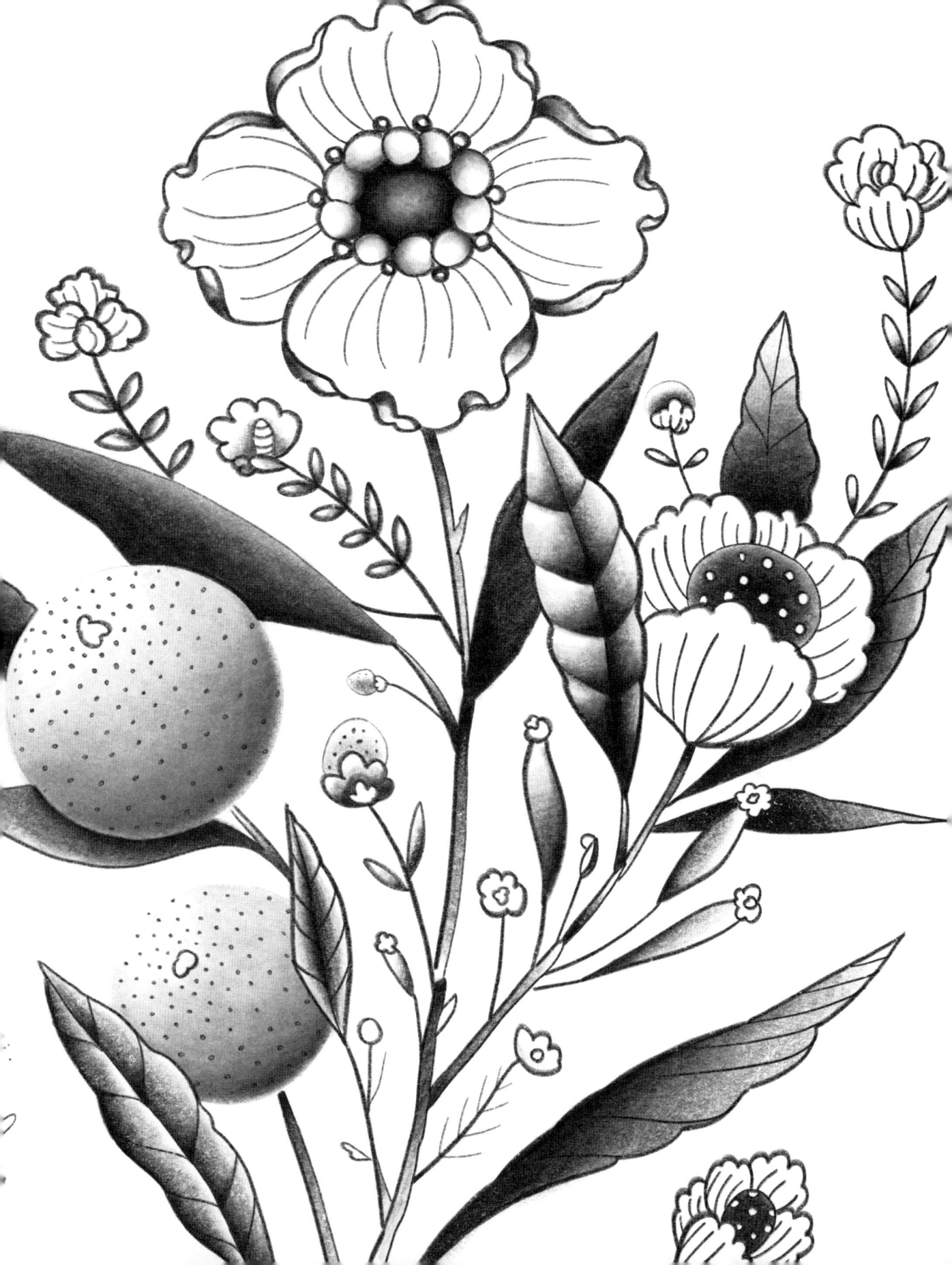

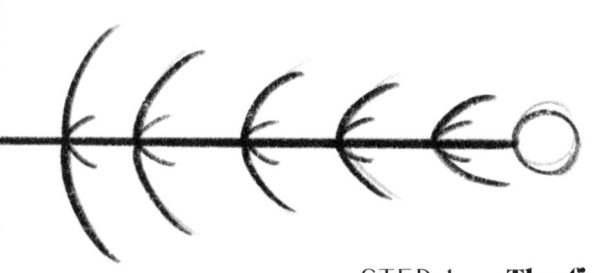
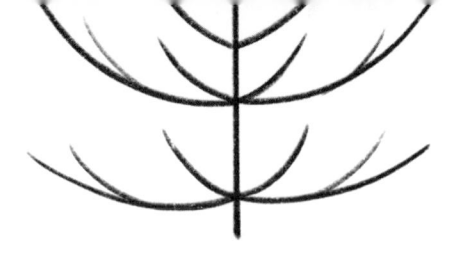

STEP 1: ESTABLISHING MOOD AND STRUCTURE

The first step is to decide what emotion you want your arrangement to carry. Once you have that in mind, let your lines respond to it.

Watch what emerges as you move your pencil. Do the lines settle into something steady and strong or drift into lighter, flowing shapes? Do they cluster close together or open out into spacious forms? These small spontaneous choices will begin to give your composition its character.

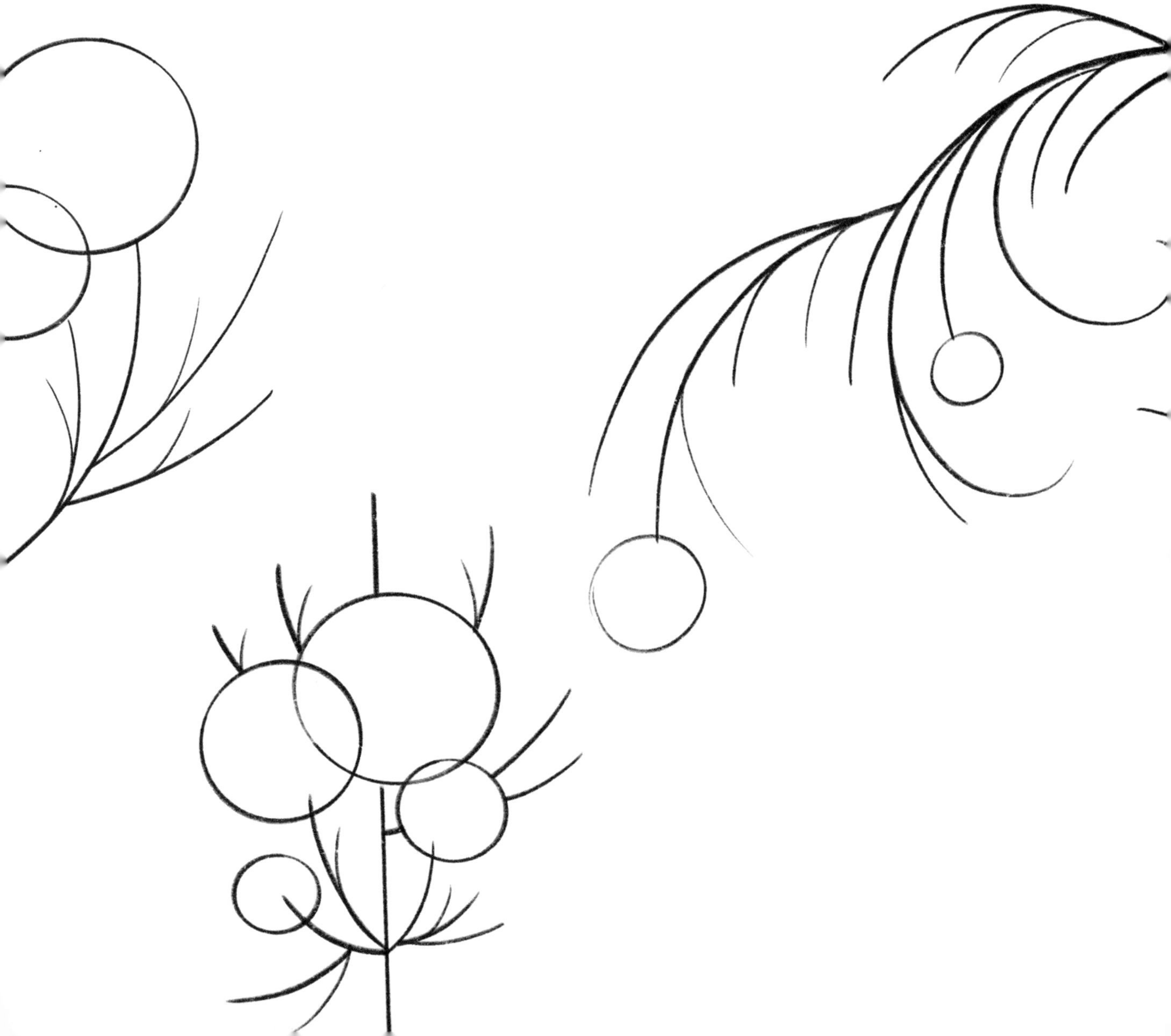

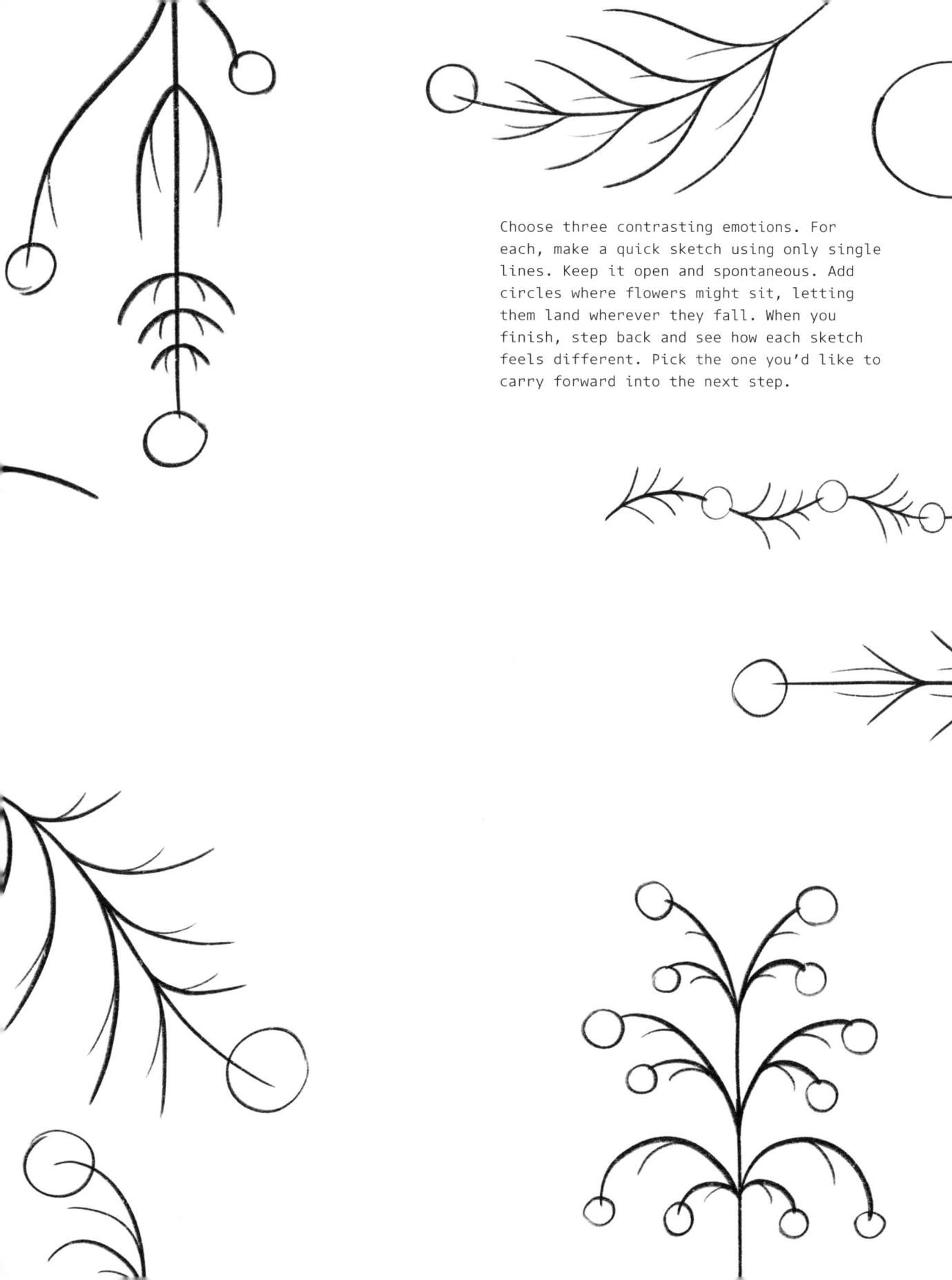

Choose three contrasting emotions. For each, make a quick sketch using only single lines. Keep it open and spontaneous. Add circles where flowers might sit, letting them land wherever they fall. When you finish, step back and see how each sketch feels different. Pick the one you'd like to carry forward into the next step.

STEP 2: LEAVES AND MOVEMENT

Leaves give rhythm to your drawing, linking flowers and stems into a whole.

Many spiky leaves scattered across a page will feel very different from long, smooth curves that flow softly through the composition. Because they repeat across the arrangement, their silhouette says a lot about the overall design. Each variation changes the overall character of the piece. By shifting their size, direction or details, your drawing grows richer in meaning.

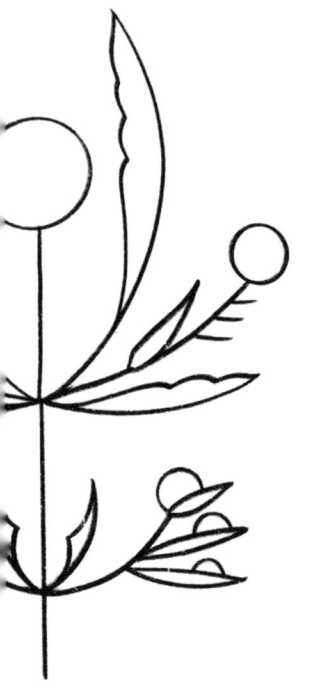

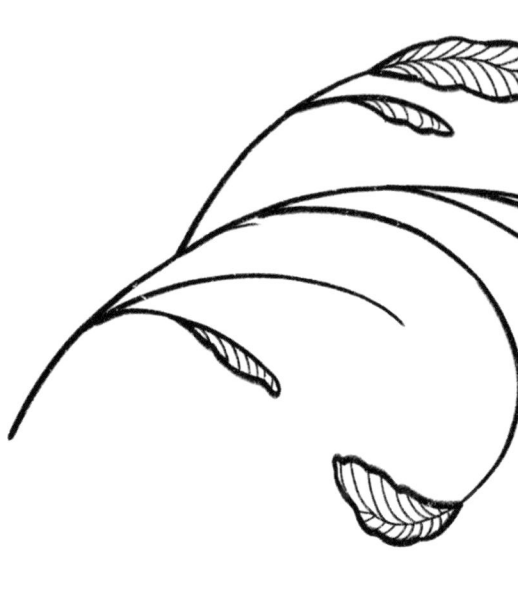

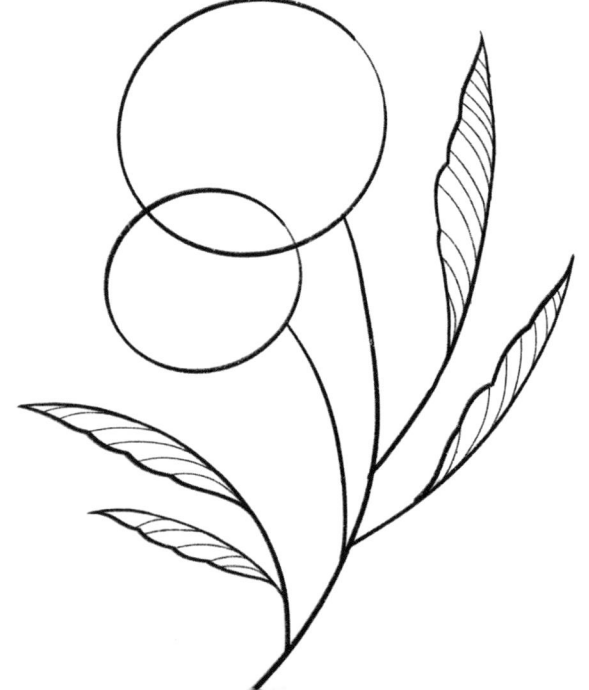

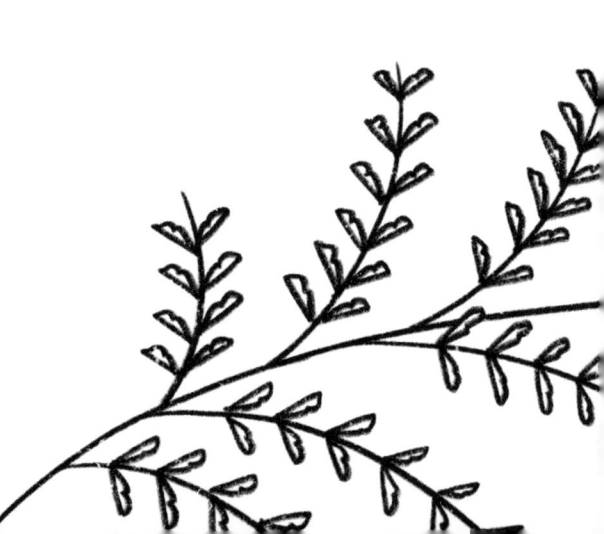

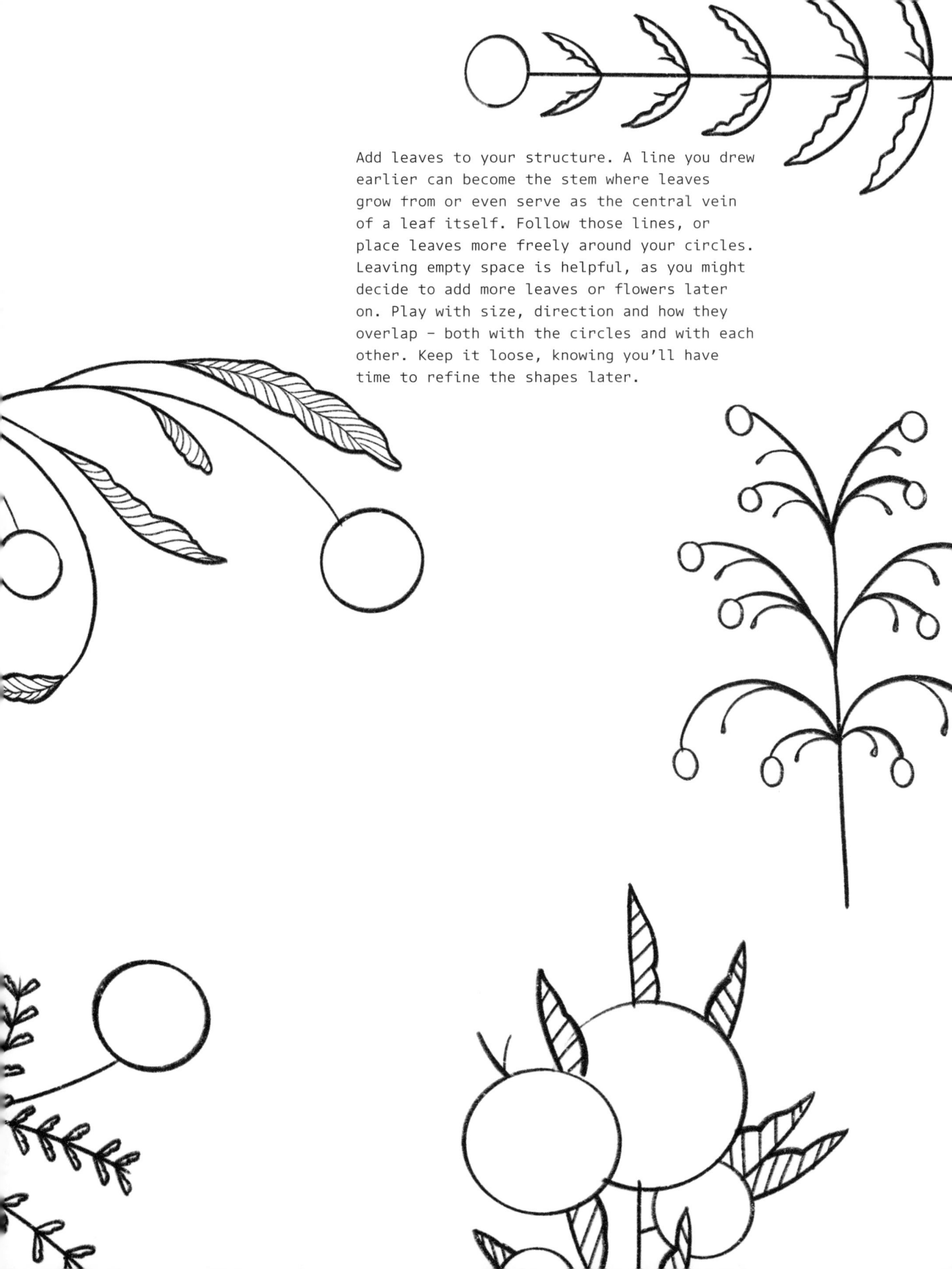

Add leaves to your structure. A line you drew
earlier can become the stem where leaves
grow from or even serve as the central vein
of a leaf itself. Follow those lines, or
place leaves more freely around your circles.
Leaving empty space is helpful, as you might
decide to add more leaves or flowers later
on. Play with size, direction and how they
overlap – both with the circles and with each
other. Keep it loose, knowing you'll have
time to refine the shapes later.

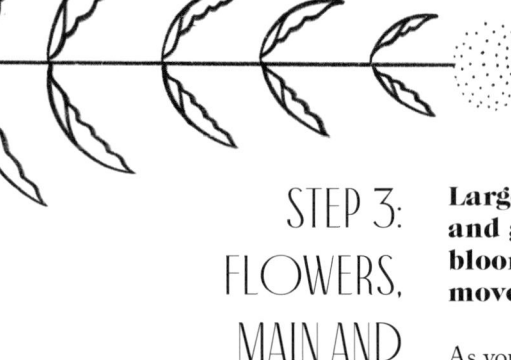

STEP 3: FLOWERS, MAIN AND SECONDARY BLOOMS

Larger flowers act as focal points, drawing the eye and giving your piece a strong presence. Smaller blooms bring variety, filling the spaces with movement and sparking interest.

As you decide on your flowers, a network of connections starts to grow across the page. A composition made with only one type of flower feels very different from one that combines many. Flowers can be simple or intricate, delicate or strong. By mindfully choosing these combinations, your arrangement comes to life.

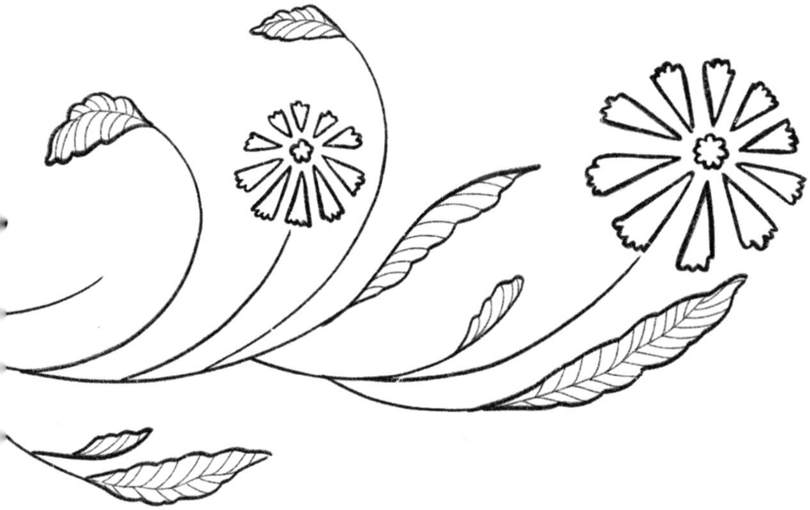

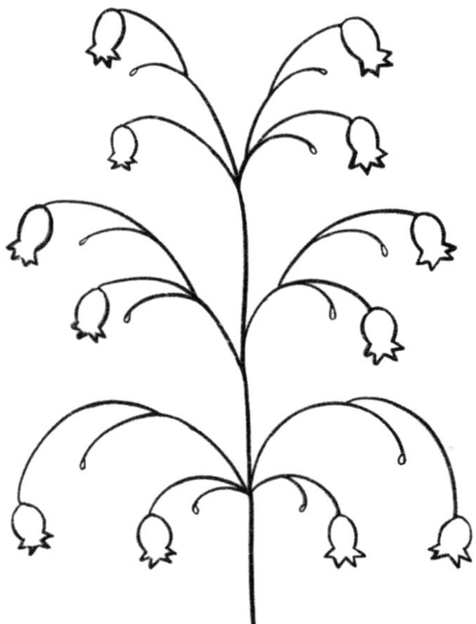

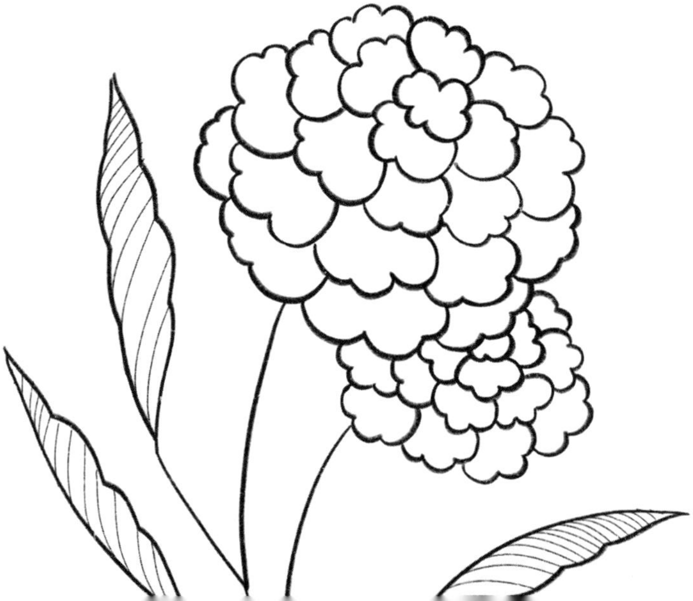

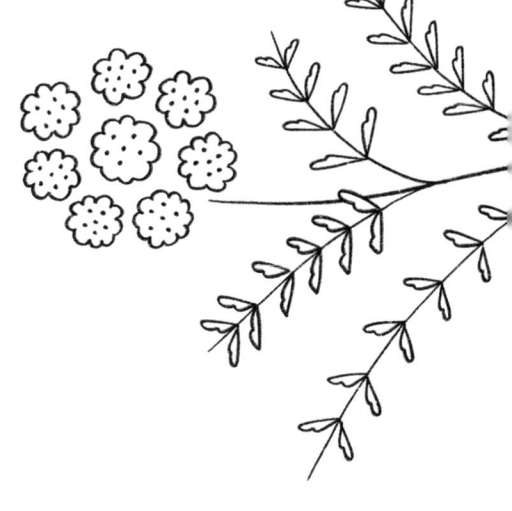

Begin to sketch your chosen flowers inside the circles
you drew earlier. Play with the orientation of each bloom
and how it relates to the others. Decide whether your
arrangement will have a clear focal point or an even spread
of attention. You can adjust the size of your circles or
draw new ones if it helps you visualize this step better.
Let some flowers or leaves overlap to bring a sense of
depth and interaction.

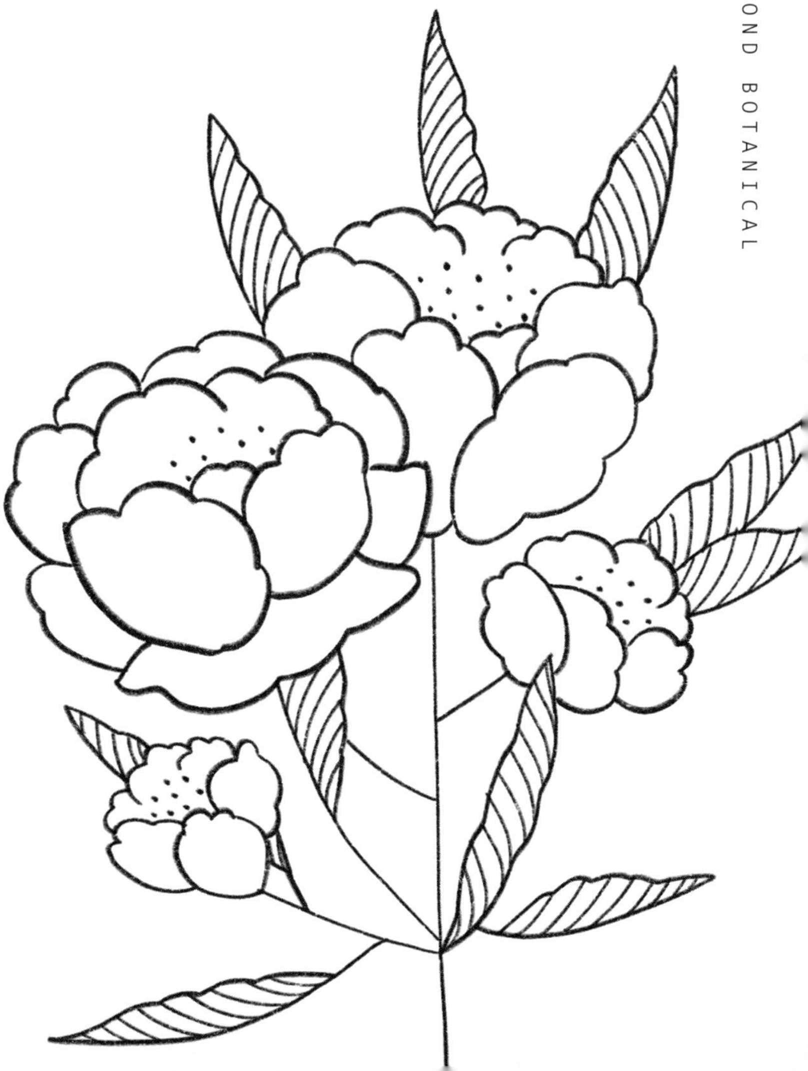

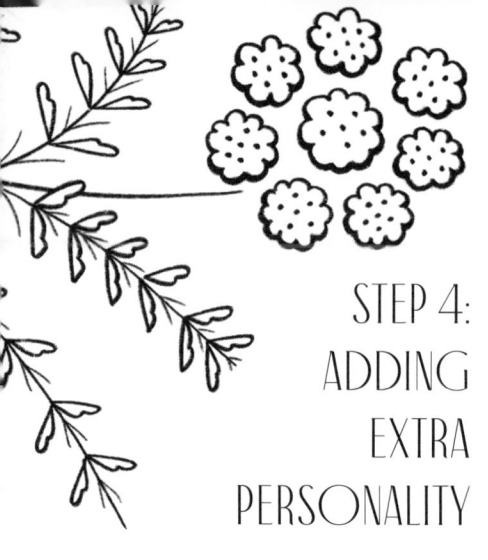

STEP 4: ADDING EXTRA PERSONALITY

Flowers and leaves set the tone of your drawing, but it's the small details that add new layers to your composition.

An unexpected curve in the stem, a thorn, a broken leaf, roots that stretch too far or petals beginning to wilt – each of these can hint at hidden stories and reveal something more about you. They draw the viewer to look more closely, encouraging them to discover a whole new dimension of detail and meaning in your drawing.

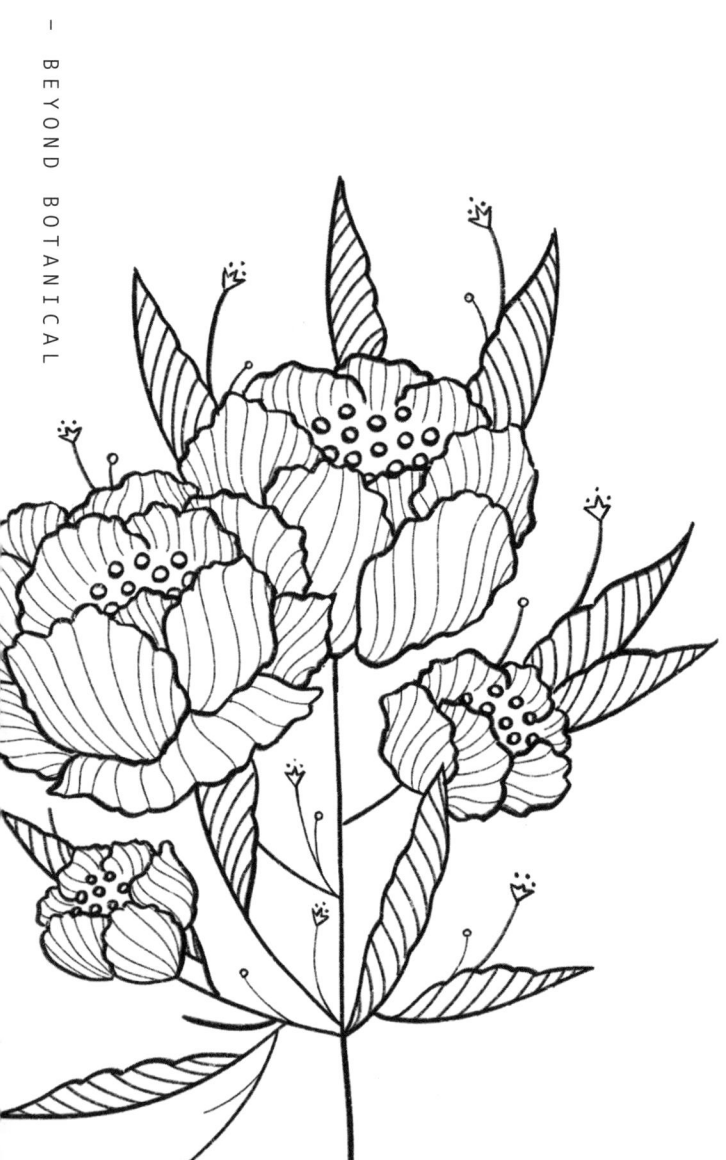

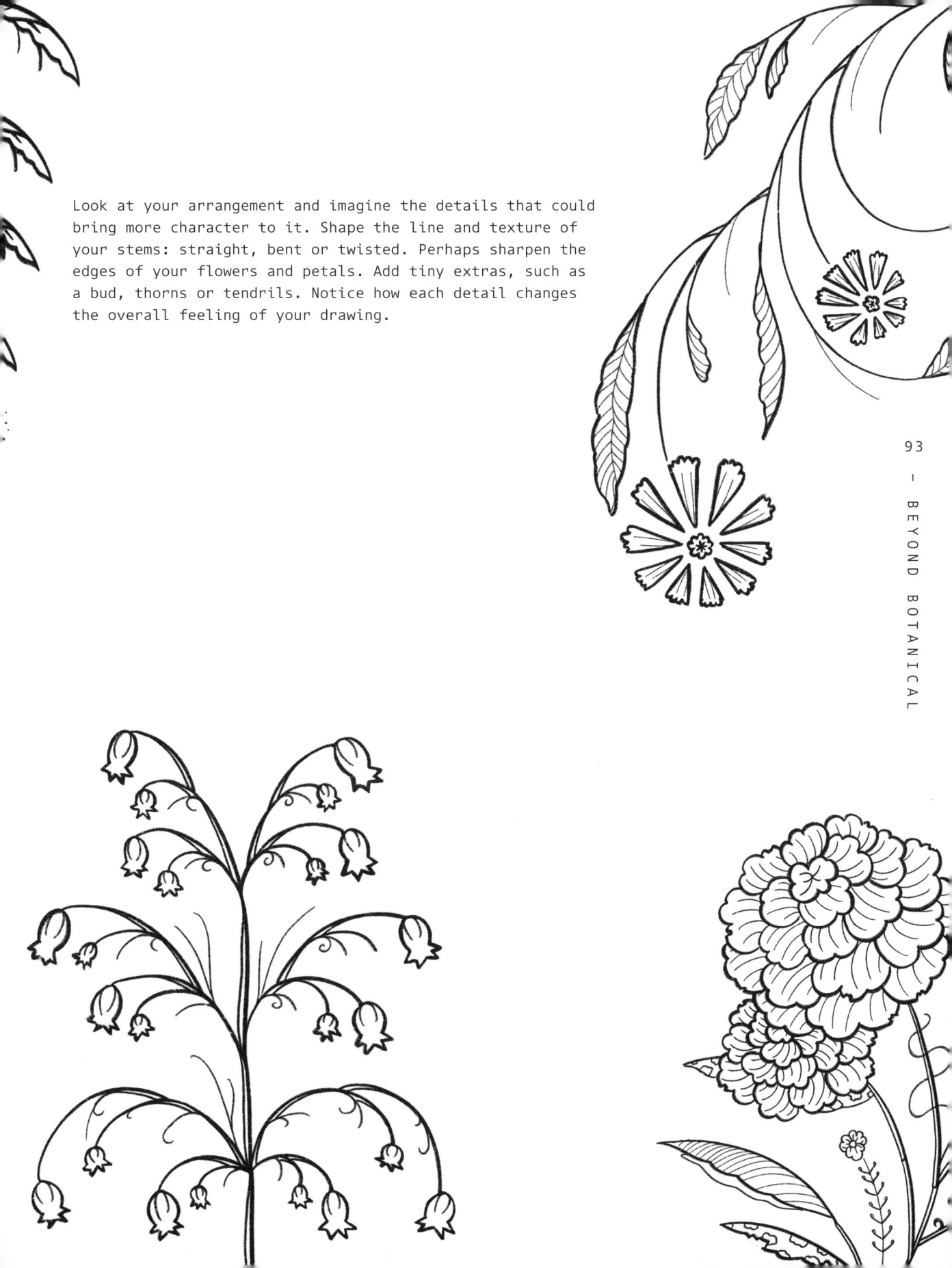

Look at your arrangement and imagine the details that could bring more character to it. Shape the line and texture of your stems: straight, bent or twisted. Perhaps sharpen the edges of your flowers and petals. Add tiny extras, such as a bud, thorns or tendrils. Notice how each detail changes the overall feeling of your drawing.

STEP 5: SHADING AND FINAL TOUCHES

Once your arrangement feels complete, take a moment to picture how light and shadow might move across it.

A good place to begin is with the leaves, since they structure the composition and help frame the flowers they surround. Another approach is to shade the darker areas first and leave the brighter ones until the end. Even small shifts between light and dark will give your drawing more presence. Shading gradually transforms the mood of your arrangement, adding depth and atmosphere to the whole piece.

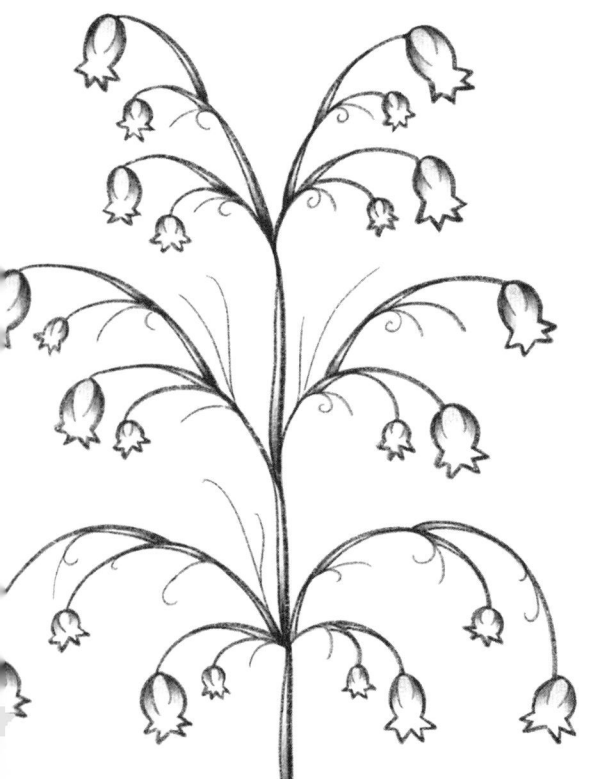

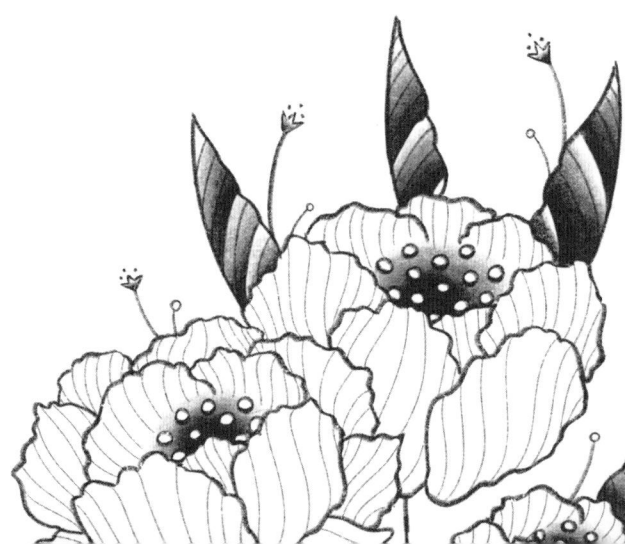

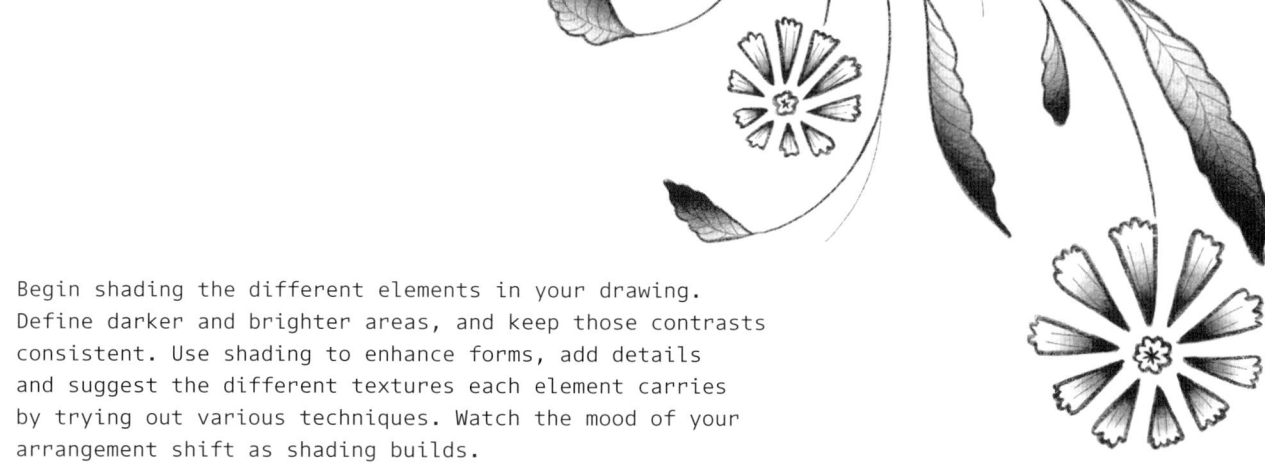

Begin shading the different elements in your drawing.
Define darker and brighter areas, and keep those contrasts
consistent. Use shading to enhance forms, add details
and suggest the different textures each element carries
by trying out various techniques. Watch the mood of your
arrangement shift as shading builds.

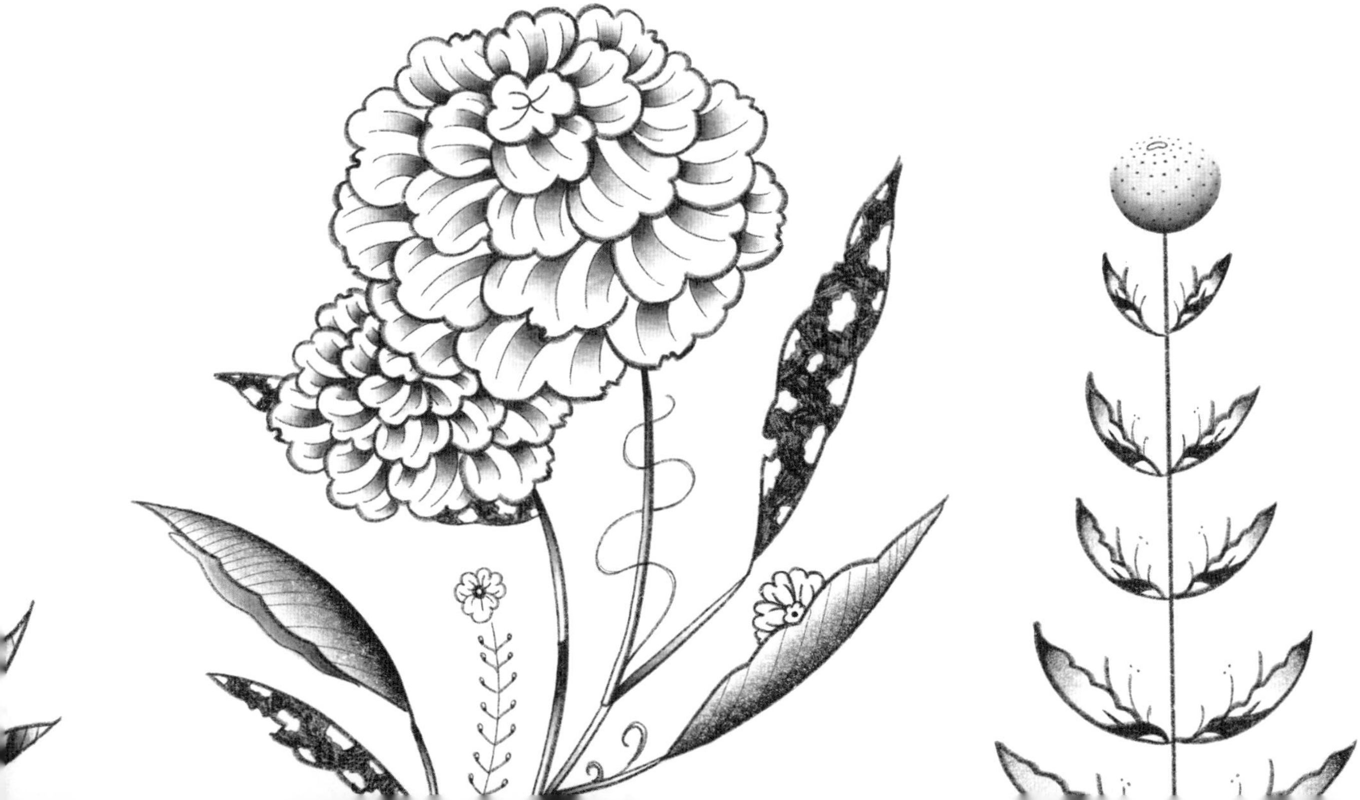

COMPOSITION CHECKLIST

Stepping back and questioning your illustration is a simple way to guide it in the direction you want.

You can use this list before committing to the next phase in your illustration, such as shading or adding detail, or afterward to reflect on what worked and what could be carried into future pieces.

Remember, it is always easier to refine early than to fix a fully developed composition. The following questions are designed to help you revisit the key aspects discussed in earlier sections of this book.

1. Does this piece reflect the mood or emotion I wanted to evoke?

2. Where do my eyes go first, and does the composition guide them smoothly?

3. Is it clear what the main subject is, or do all elements compete equally for attention?

4. How do the flowers and leaves relate to each other? Do their orientations create a sense of connection and interaction?

5. How do the spaces between elements feel, and do they create balance and rhythm in the flow?

6. Are some elements overlapping in a way that adds depth, or could certain layers be adjusted for more dimension?

7. Do the proportions between stems, leaves and flowers feel balanced and harmonious, or does something dominate too much?

8. Is there enough variety in stages of growth to make the arrangement feel alive?

9. Do repeated shapes create balance without becoming monotonous, and is there enough variety to keep it engaging?

10. Does the composition feel lively and natural, or could some areas be softened or adjusted?

EMOTIONAL CHECK-IN

Taking a moment to reflect on how drawing feels is a simple way to stay in touch with yourself and notice what supports you along your creative process.

This list can be used at any stage, whether you are in the middle of a piece or looking back once it feels complete, to pause and notice the moments that stood out and the choices that shaped your experience.

These questions focus less on technical decisions and more on your mood, attention and enjoyment, so you can carry what feels most meaningful into future compositions.

1. What is my favourite moment in this composition?

2. How did the process feel? Calm, playful, challenging or something else?

3. What did I enjoy most while making this piece?

4. Which techniques felt most rewarding to use?

5. Which decisions had the greatest influence on how the piece turned out?

6. Did I give myself enough time and space to explore ideas, or did I move too quickly?

7. What surprised me during the process?

8. Which aspects of this composition would I like to carry forward into a future piece?

9. If I could adjust one part of this piece, what would it be, and why?

10. What might I approach differently in my next composition?

LET THIS SPACE GATHER ANY THOUGHTS OR IDEAS THAT SURFACED ALONG THIS PROCESS:

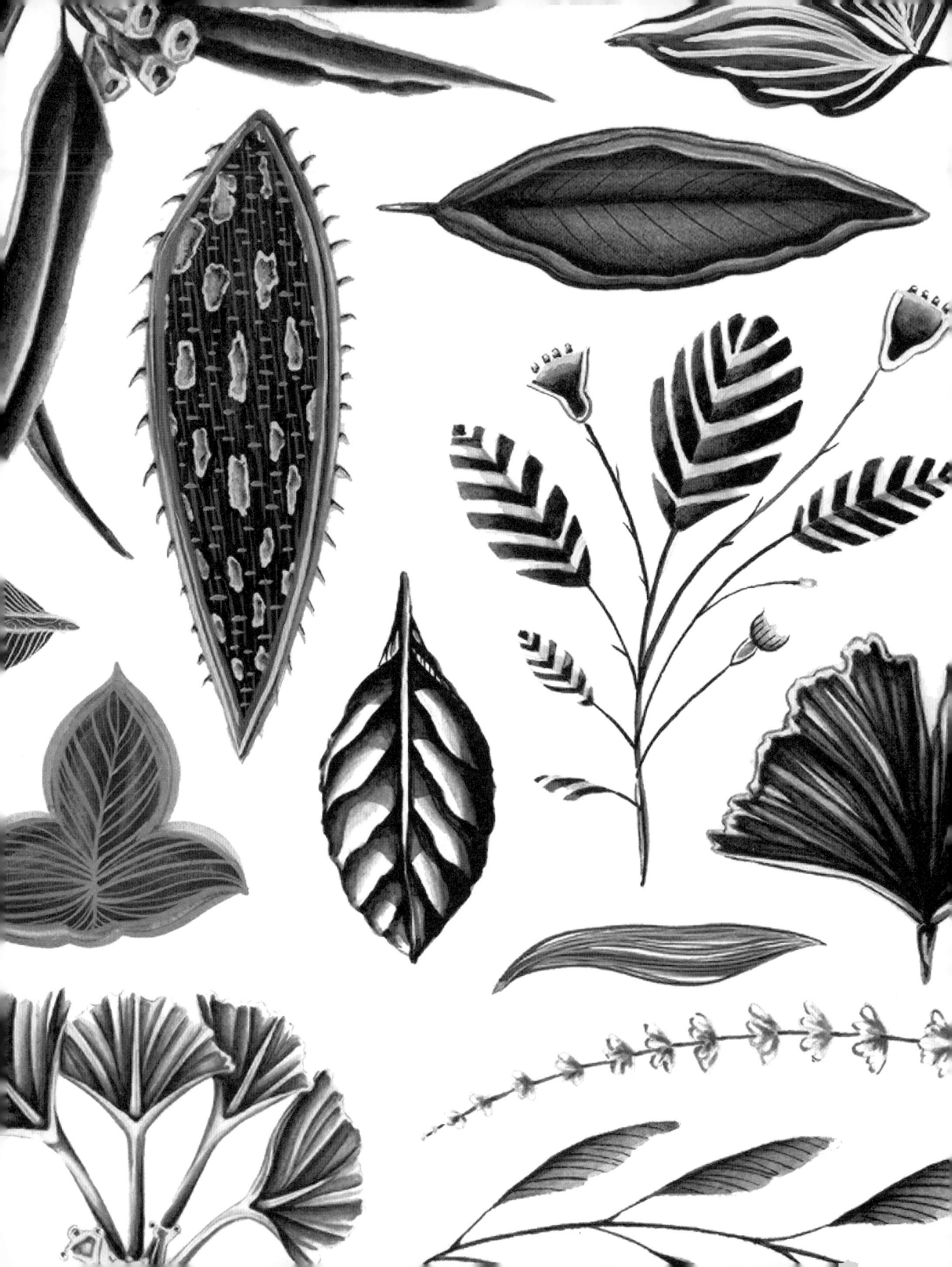

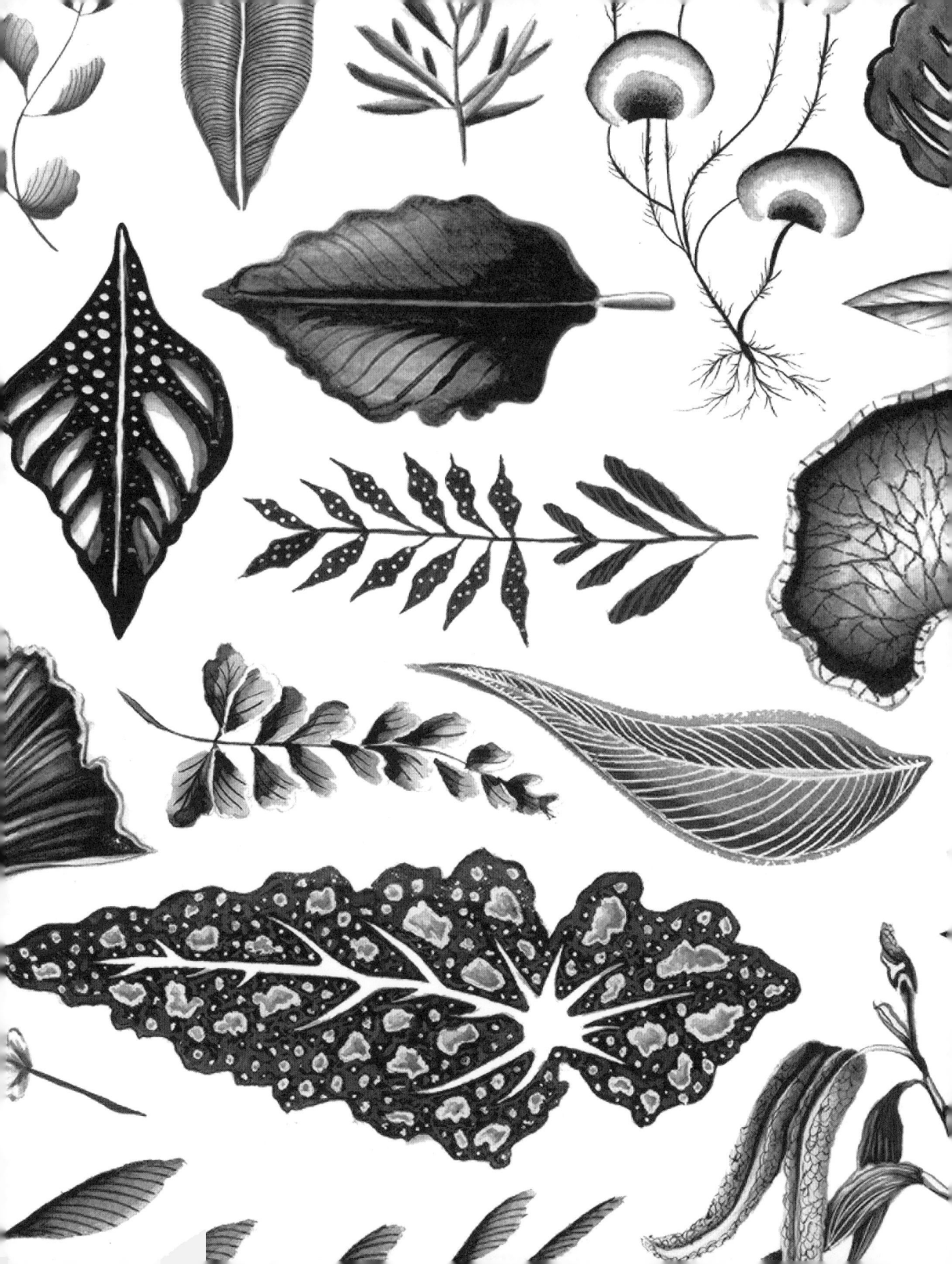

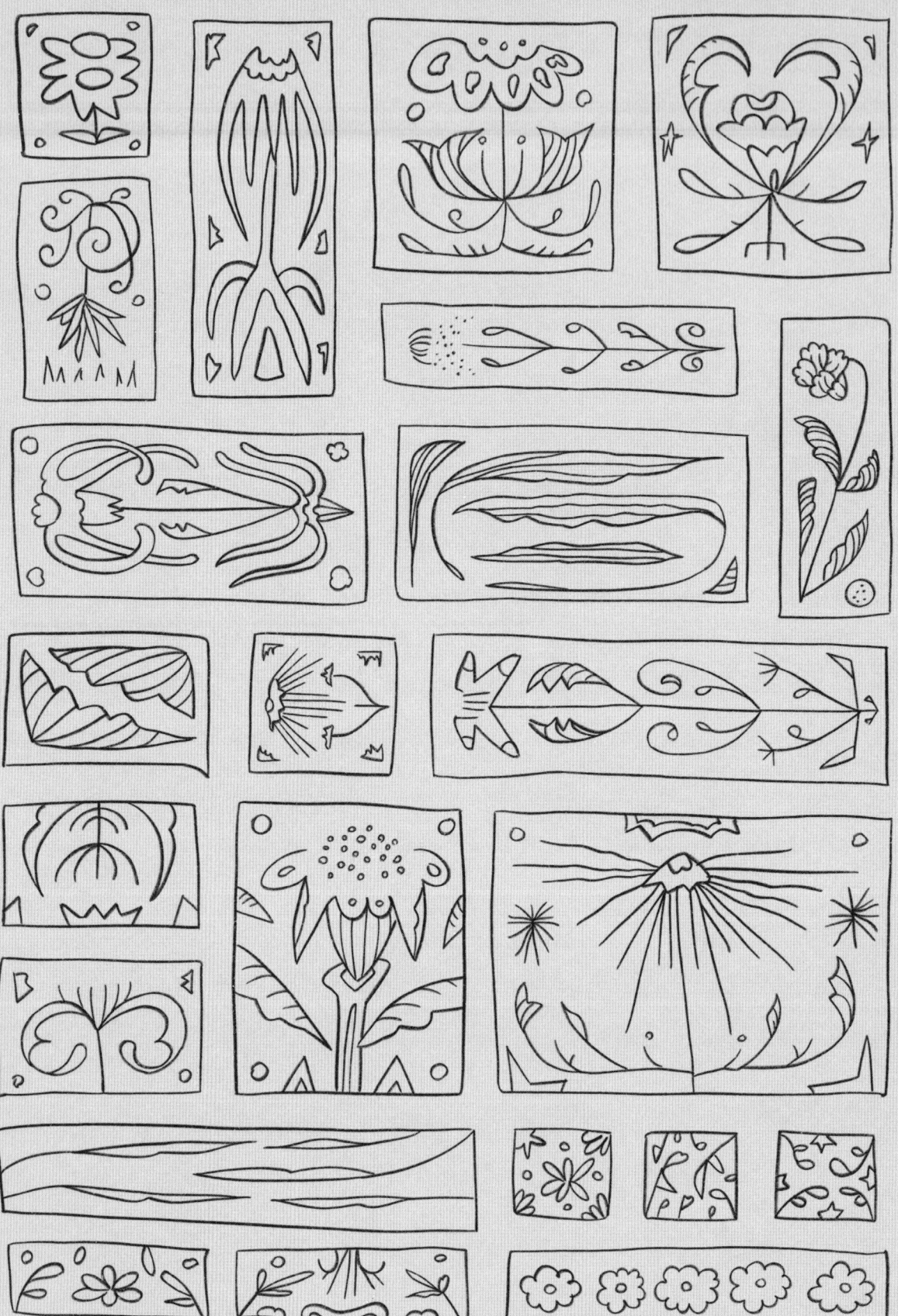

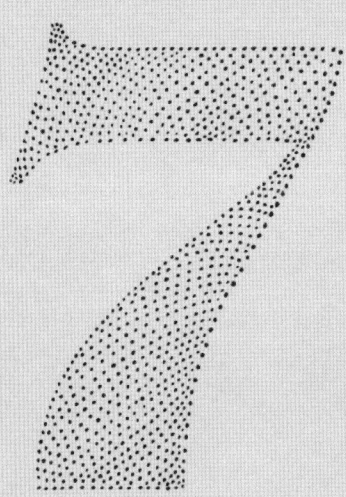

BEYOND BOTANICAL

Welcome to my favourite chapter of this book.

Here we approach the practice of drawing plants in a new way. Over the years I've noticed that the more I open myself to plants, the more they share with me.

To truly learn from them, you need to shift from being an observer to being fully present in their company. When you meet a plant as a living being, just as alive as you are, it begins to reveal itself differently.

Often there's an invisible hierarchy between ourselves and what we draw; we sit before it as an observer, and the plant becomes 'the thing' we are drawing. Yet they are very much alive, and to represent this in your artwork you need to tune into that reality.

The simplest way – and also the most challenging – is to temporarily set aside everything you know about yourself: your name, where you live, friends and even the things you like the most.

The more we hold onto ourselves, the less space there is to experience others, including plants. Meet a plant simply as one living being encountering another, and you'll find much more to see.

So, I invite you to slip out of your human suit for a moment and come with me.

BEYOND WORDS: HOW TO TALK WITH PLANTS

Our connection with plants goes beyond watering schedules and sunlight. Like any friendship, it grows through attention, care and shared moments.

This exercise invites you to start conversations with your indoor plants, strengthening your bond in ways that might surprise you. At first, it may feel like a one-way street, but before long you'll notice that plants have their own ways of responding. Whether you're already an experienced plant-chatter or just testing the waters, these steps will help turn your houseplants into trusted companions.

STEP 1: BREAKING THE ICE
Start with a plant that already feels familiar, maybe one you've grown from a cutting or received as a gift – we all have our favourites! Keep it simple; a quick greeting is enough for now. Even the shyest plant appreciates a little acknowledgement.

STEP 2: CHEERING ON NEW GROWTH
Plants, just like anyone else, thrive on kind words. If you spot a new sprout or unfolding leaf, a small compliment goes a long way. A simple 'That new leaf looks amazing on you', or 'Can't wait to see that bud bloom' might just make their day.

STEP 3: NAMING WITH LOVE
Giving your plant a name (or a nickname) adds familiarity. After all, you wouldn't want to share your home with strangers. You might ask, 'What would you like to be called?' and trust that the answer will come to you in time. Don't forget to introduce yourself too!

STEP 4: NURTURING THE BOND
Friendships grow through understanding. Pay attention to your plant's preferences – maybe it enjoys a misty morning spritz or prefers a cozy spot in the shade. You might wonder aloud, 'Would you like more sunlight?' or 'How about a bigger pot for extra space?'. These small acts of care will strengthen your relationship.

STEP 5: ESTABLISHING RITUALS

As with any friendship, spending quality time together deepens the connection. Maybe you dedicate a weekly 'Plant Care Day' to watering, dusting leaves or giving your plant a gentle shower. A simple 'It's our care day!' turns routine maintenance into something special, making your plant feel like a true part of your life.

STEP 6: OPENING UP

As your connection grows, share more of yourself. Tell your plant about your first houseplant disaster, or that time you spotted a rare flower on a hike. Friendships are built on shared experiences, so letting them in on your stories makes the relationship feel more natural.

STEP 7: SPENDING MOMENTS TOGETHER

Beyond tending to their needs, simply being with your plant matters. Sit nearby while drinking tea, read them an interesting passage from your book, play them your favourite album or just enjoy a quiet moment in their company. Over time, their presence becomes part of your daily rhythm, something to return to and find comfort in.

STEP 8: BEING VULNERABLE

Plants listen without judgement. You might find yourself sharing small hopes or even secrets you wouldn't dare tell another person. Whether it's a big dream or just a passing thought, speaking it aloud can make it feel more real. Your plant won't offer advice right away, but it will hold space for you, quietly absorbing your words as you learn more about yourself.

STEP 9: GROWING YOUR PLANT CIRCLE

Once this practice becomes second nature, extend it within and beyond your home. Say hello and goodnight to all your plants; they might feel left out otherwise. A smile at a towering tree in the park, a gentle touch to a blooming flower, a nod to a vine curling along a fence … every small interaction counts. Before you know it, even unknown places will begin to feel a little more familiar, as if plants growing there are already waiting to meet you.

AS YOUR RELATIONSHIP WITH YOUR PLANTS GROWS, USE THIS SPACE TO NOTE ANY NEW DISCOVERIES, THOUGHTS OR SMALL CHANGES YOU'VE OBSERVED.

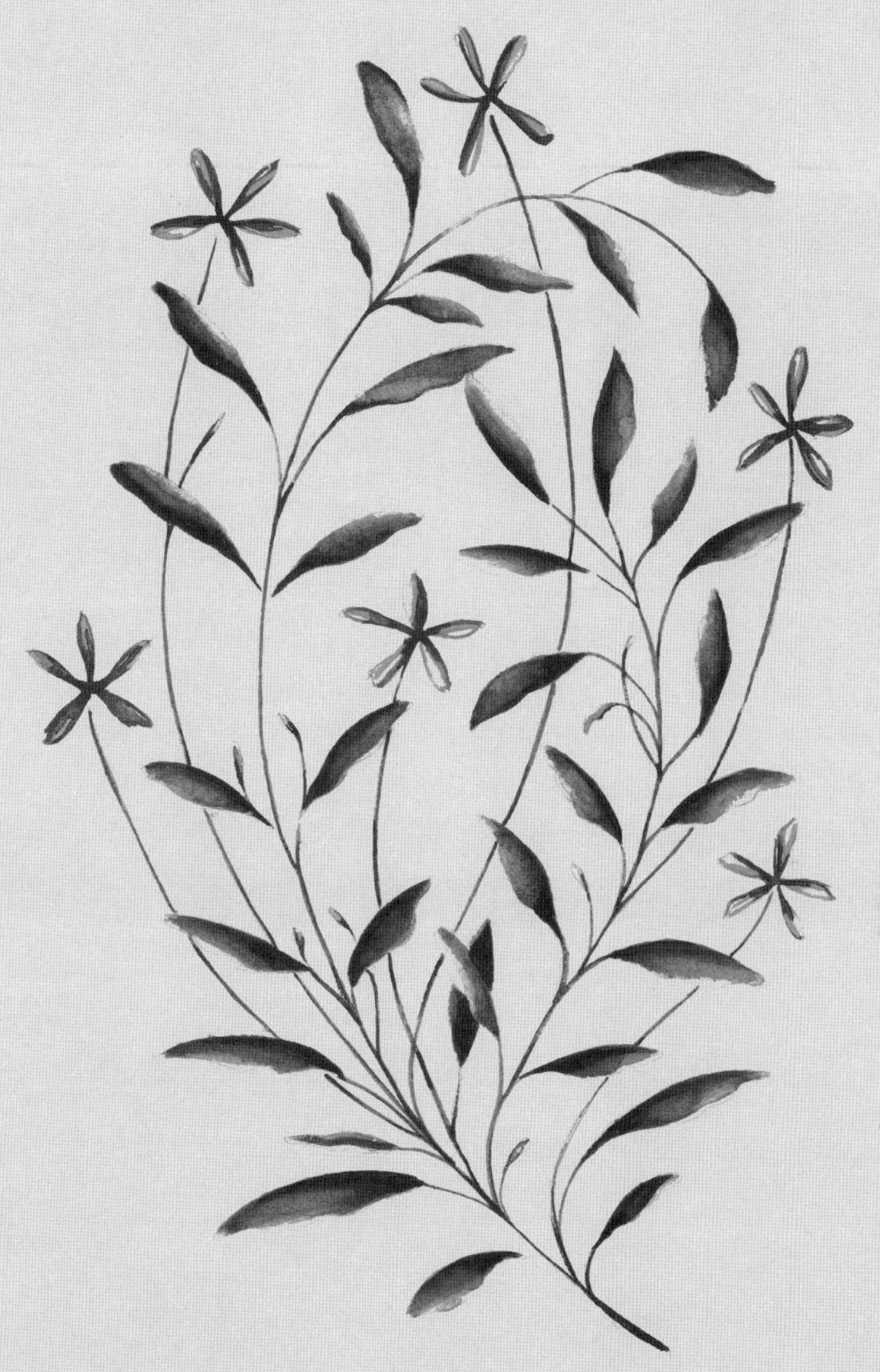

BEYOND PERSPECTIVE: HOW TO DRAW LIKE A PLANT

Have you ever imagined the world from a plant's point of view, rooted in one place through every season, sensing through light, touch and the air around it?

In this exercise, we'll explore what it might be like to draw from your plant's perspective, tapping into its unique sensory realm.

SETTING

Change into your comfiest outfit and find a quiet, cozy spot in your home. Gather markers, pencils or any medium you enjoy. Dim the overhead lights, letting soft lamps or candles create a gentle glow. Brew your favourite herbal tea, settle into a comfy seat and play some instrumental music in the background.

ENQUIRE

Pick a plant you feel drawn to. Sit facing it with a soft gaze, then close your eyes and gently touch it as you consider the following questions:

• If this plant were to draw me, what would I look like?
• How might it perceive my shape, colours and presence?
• Does it sense temperature, sound or movement?

JOURNAL

Open your eyes and take a moment to journal your thoughts. Use any space on these pages to write down whatever comes to mind as you consider how your plant perceives you.

DRAW AS A PLANT WOULD

Use the space across these pages for your drawing. Reflect on the prompts below for inspiration:

• Imagine your plant seeing only in warm or cold tones.
• Consider how it might perceive subtle shifts in colour or light.
• Picture it sensing you as a swirl of energy rather than a distinct human shape.
• Focus on movement and repetition rather than precision or control.
• Notice how it might respond to your touch and to the vibrations of your voice.

Be creative and let your answers guide the marks you make on your surface. Challenge yourself to step outside your usual ways of representation. Remember, your plant doesn't have human eyes and couldn't care less about your skills!

Start drawing here. Let the impressions from your plant
influence your marks as lines and forms emerge on the page.

Give thanks to your plant for helping you see things
differently. Take a moment to look at your drawing and
notice what emerged: the shapes, colours or movements you
might not have expected. By exploring how your plant might
experience life, you can discover insights not just about
the plant, but also about your own perceptions.

BEYOND PERCEPTION: HOW TO DRAW INVISIBLE PLANTS

Drawing invisible plants might feel daunting at first, but it's simpler than you think. Step by step, I'll guide you through bringing a plant from your imagination into this world.

In this exercise, we'll follow the natural growth of a plant, moving from seed to fruit, so that each stage builds on the last. By visualizing each part on its own, you'll get a clearer sense of its form, shape, texture and colour before bringing them together into a new, unique specimen.

GETTING STARTED

Start with the prompts below and take your time with each question. Close your eyes and let your mind wander, picturing the details. If you like, write down your answers, describing whatever comes to you, or say your words aloud – sometimes hearing them can spark new images. Allow the forms to emerge and sketch what you see, piece by piece.

   As you move through this section, you'll find space to make small sketches alongside the prompts. Keep them simple: outlines, shapes or textures. These little drawings will serve as references when assembling your plant.

   Once you've explored each section, you'll be ready to bring everything together. Your answers will naturally guide the shape of your plant. Let's begin.

SEED

APPEARANCE: What does the seed look like? Is it tiny, like a poppy seed, or large, like a coconut? Is its surface smooth, rough or marked with unusual textures?

FUNCTION: What makes it sprout? Does it need a heavy rain to germinate, or does it emerge after months of resting in the soil?

FEEL: If you held it in your hand, how would it feel? Light or heavy, solid or brittle?

GROWTH: What kind of environment does this seed need? Does it thrive in desert sands, the rich soil of a forest or even underwater?

ROOTS

APPEARANCE: Are the roots a complex network spreading wide and deep, or a single strong root anchoring the plant firmly?

FUNCTION: Do they store nutrients, seek out hidden water or intertwine with other plants to share resources?

FEEL: Are they thick and rugged, thin and delicate, or perhaps covered in fine hairs? Do they grip tightly to the soil or wander loosely through it?

GROWTH: What kind of earth do the roots need? Are they buried in dense clay, loose sand or a damp forest floor?

STEM

APPEARANCE: What colour is the stem? Is it vibrant green, earthy brown or something unexpected like pale blue, fluorescent yellow or even silver? Is it thick and sturdy or slender and flexible?

FUNCTION: Does the stem support heavy blossoms, store water or climb toward the light? Does it bend easily in the wind or stay rigid?

FEEL: Is it smooth to the touch, lined with ridges or covered in soft fuzz? Does it have protective spikes or a waxy coating?

GROWTH: Does it grow straight up in the open sun, weave through dense foliage or creep across rocky terrain?

LEAVES

APPEARANCE: Are the leaves broad and flat to capture sunlight, or small and waxy to prevent moisture loss? Are they a steady green or do they shift colours with light and season?

FUNCTION: Do they provide shade, store water or release a fragrance? Do they curl in the heat or spread wide at dawn?

FEEL: Are they smooth, velvety or leathery to the touch? Do they feel fragile, thick or wax-coated? Do they release a scent when crushed?

GROWTH: Are the leaves adapted to harsh sunlight, heavy rainfall, biting winds or cold nights?

BRANCHES

APPEARANCE: How do the branches grow from the stem? Do they form a dense canopy, spread wide and open or spiral and fork in surprising ways?

FUNCTION: Do they support leaves and flowers, reach toward the sun or offer a resting place for animals and insects?

FEEL: Are they smooth and firm, rough and knotted or covered in peeling bark? Do they sway easily in the wind or stand unyielding?

GROWTH: Are the branches shaped by constant sunlight, heavy humidity or the force of strong winds?

FLOWERS

APPEARANCE: Are the flowers large and bold or small and delicate? Do they blaze with colour, glow softly or carry patterns like spots, stripes or gradated colour?

FUNCTION: How often do they bloom? Do they open only in the morning, after rain or once in many years? Do they attract pollinators?

FEEL: Are the petals silky and soft, crisp as paper or thick and rubbery? Do they release a fragrance or feel cool against your skin?

GROWTH: Do the flowers thrive only in bright sun, bloom only in deep shade or wait for a particular season to appear?

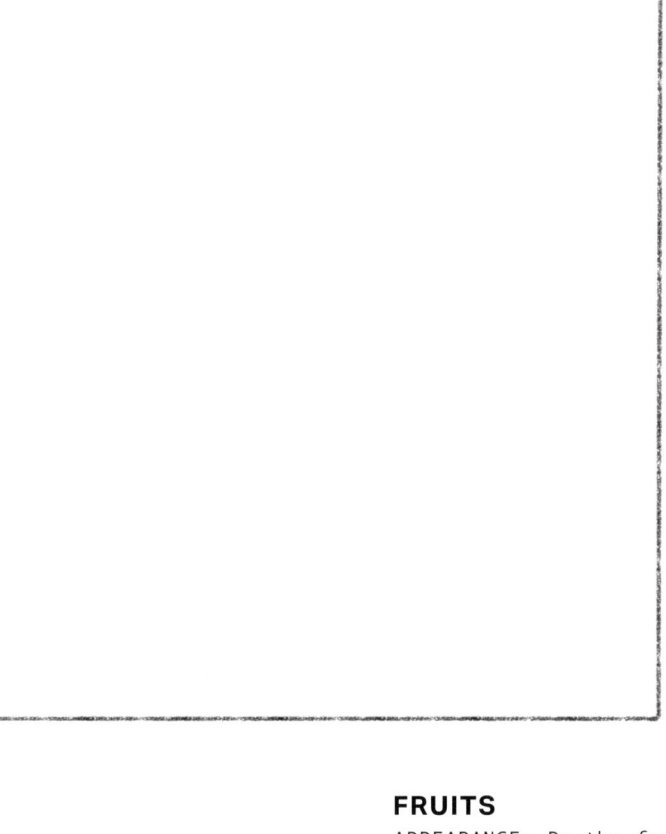

FRUITS

APPEARANCE: Do the fruits resemble something you know, or do they take on wild new forms? Are they rounded, spiky, stretched long or even hollow?

FUNCTION: When do they appear? Once a year, with every new moon or only after a special event? Do they nourish animals or carry seeds far from the plant?

FEEL: Are they firm and crisp, soft and juicy or sealed within a tough shell? Do they smell sweet, sharp or entirely unfamiliar?

GROWTH: Do the fruits ripen in hot, humid climates, require dry conditions or appear only in a certain season?

ASSEMBLING YOUR PLANT

Now that you've explored each part of your plant, it's time to bring everything together. Imagine you're assembling a puzzle, where each element you've created helps shape the final form.

Look back at the small sketches you drew for each part, and any notes you made. Together they already give you the beginnings of a plant. Do any patterns or connections stand out?

SKETCH A ROUGH OUTLINE.

Before refining the details, make a simple drawing of your plant as a whole. Don't worry about perfection, just let the overall shape emerge.

CONSIDER HOW THE PARTS INTERACT.

- How do the roots support the stem?
- How do the branches and leaves affect the plant's balance? If it has flowers and fruits, what role do they play in the design?

PLAY WITH COMBINATIONS.

If something feels off, adjust it. Maybe your plant has no branches, or its flowers grow directly from the roots. There are no rules; follow whatever comes to you.

REFINE AND FINALIZE.

Once you have a full picture, add the finishing details, then use the space provided to draw your complete plant — and give it a name, if you'd like.

Use this area to bring your plant together. Let your imagination go wild and enjoy the process of creating something entirely new and unique. If you want a little nudge, you can refer to my example on the next page.

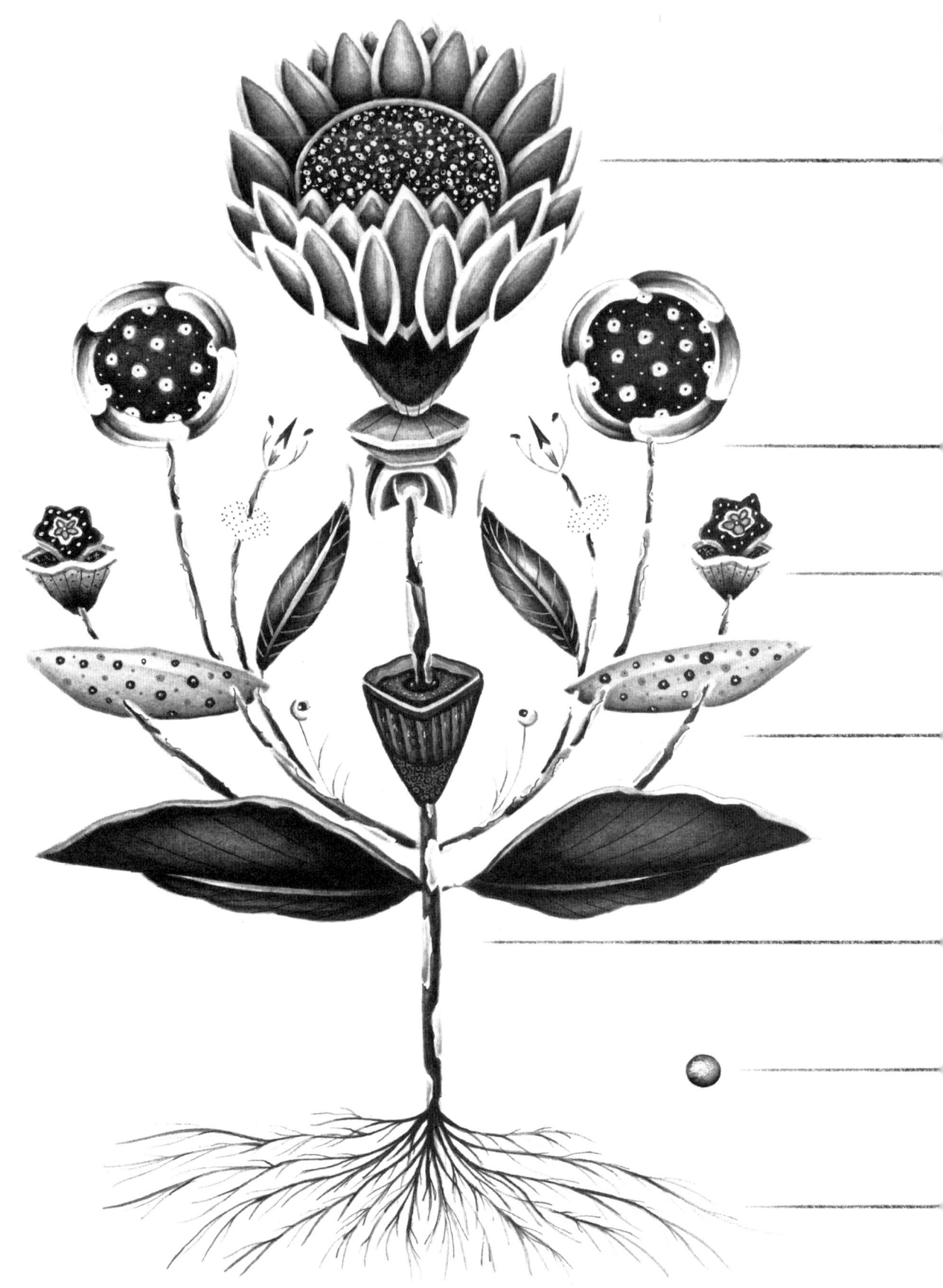

FLOWER

Large, layered, geometric bloom. Opens one night a year under the equinox full moon.

This plant inhabits the salt deserts, where the ground is cracked, dry and nearly sterile. Its life begins with a pearlescent seed that waits a full year in stillness before blooming for one night under the equinox full moon. Roots draw minerals from the crust and the air, aided by branches that sense humidity and harvest particles. A tall, black stem holds veined and silvery leaves, forming an aerodynamic structure around the bloom. The flower is large and geometric, opening only under precise conditions. Its star-shaped fruit, creamy within, is carried across the flats only by the white desert fox, ensuring the cycle continues.

BRANCHES

Symmetrical, ordered pattern: fruit-bearing, air-sensing, and mineral-harvesting.

FRUIT

Star-shaped shell. Creamy interior. Carried only by the desert fox.

LEAVES

Two types: thick dark veined leaves release a repellent scent; thin silvery leaves reinforce aerodynamic structure.

STEM

Tall, black stem with white specks. Architectural and upright, built to endure harsh winds.

SEED

Pearlescent sphere. Paper-thin skin. Sprouts only after seasonal rains. Waits a full year before bloom.

ROOTS

Filaments dissolve at touch. Absorb minerals from salt crust and fleeting desert moisture.

BEYOND QUESTIONS: HOW TO HEAR WHAT PLANTS HAVE TO SAY

Have you ever wondered what your plant might say if it could speak? Or what it might be thinking about? In this section, we'll explore how asking questions can bring new depth to your drawings.

The answers you receive will guide you toward new pathways of representing the plants around you.

A CONVERSATION STARTER

Pick a plant you feel drawn to – maybe one you've had for years, or a new one you've just discovered. Before you begin drawing, use any space on these pages to reflect on the questions that follow. Keep it spontaneous, don't overthink, just let whatever comes to mind land on the page.

1. If your plant could move, where would it go?

2. If your plant could speak, what would it say to you?

3. If your plant could hear you, what would you say to it?

4. If your plant could dream, what would it dream about?

5. If your plant had one big wish, what would it be?

6. If your plant were a different colour, what colour would it be?

7. If your plant could make a sound, what would it be?

8. If your plant had a taste, what would it taste like?

9. If your plant could interact with other plants, what would it do?

10. If your plant could remember, what would it recall?

A MOMENT OF REFLECTION

Once you've answered these questions, pause to reflect on what you've written. How do you feel about your plant now? Has your perception shifted? Does it seem more alive, more present? Or perhaps more mysterious?

Here is where your drawing begins; let your answers guide you. Maybe your plant takes on the colour of its dreams, or its shape shifts to match the sound you imagined. Use these insights to shape how you bring it to life.

BEYOND SEPARATION: HOW TO BECOME THE FOREST

Before we begin, I need to warn you, becoming the forest takes time. If you find yourself impatient, start with simpler steps, like how to talk with plants or how to hear what plants have to say. Those exercises are easier to approach and will gradually lead you there.

As humans, we often treat nature like it's just scenery, something in the background of our lives. Yet trees, rivers, mountains and even rocks have been offering us a sense of kinship and home since the beginning of time, shaping our wellbeing and ways of gathering for countless generations.

To become the forest, the most important step is to question what is separating you from it right now. What is stopping you from feeling more like a bird or a tree? Is it the way you move through the world? The way you think about nature? Have you learned to see it as something apart from you? Start by walking in the forest, breathing its air, sleeping under its canopy and learning its stories. Learn about the plants around you – bluebell, heather, daffodil. They all existed even before we could label them. Names are just ways we navigate space; let go of what keeps you held apart.

Try to connect with how everything has its place in the ecosystem, coexisting in balance – even yourself. Observe how every element – plants, animals, air and soil – contributes to a larger harmony. The more you notice, the more you understand that you too have a place in this balance.

Little by little you'll feel more at home, closer to it, part of it. When you go on a walk in the forest, you might say, 'Thank you for letting me enjoy you.' And when you leave, 'Thank you for this beautiful moment. See you soon.' Over time, these small gestures grow into a relationship of mutual recognition. You'll sense yourself becoming a bit more forest each day.

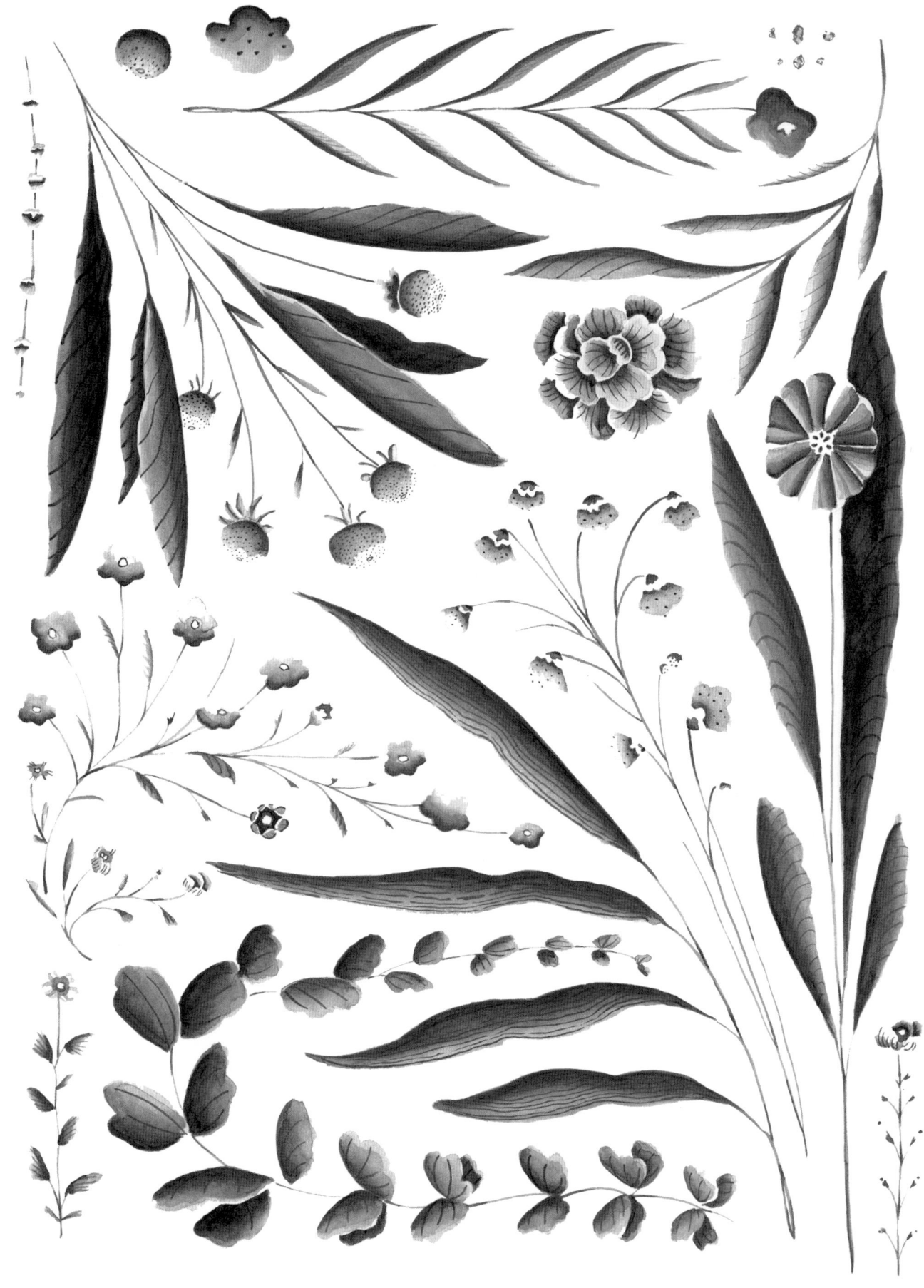

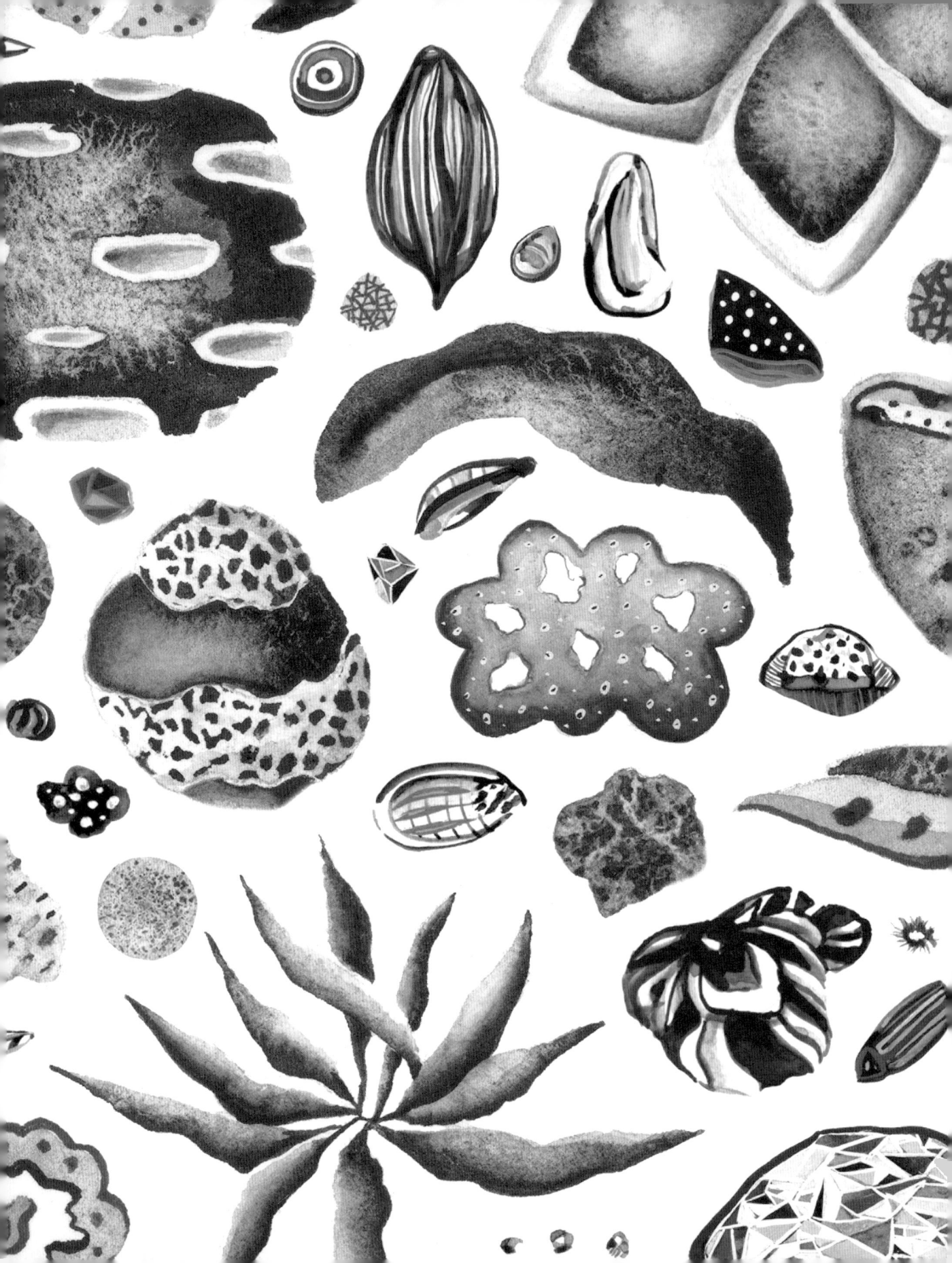

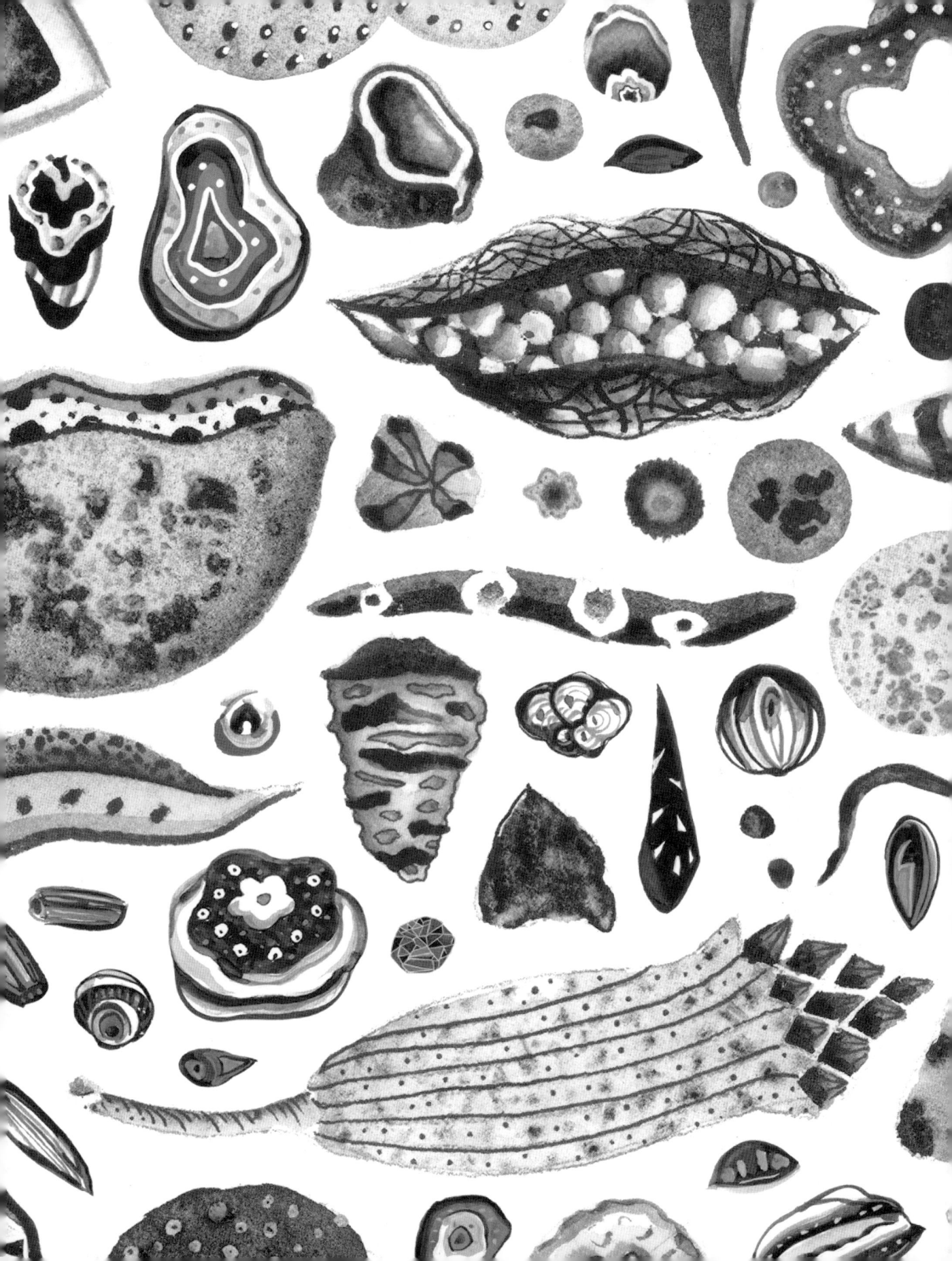

AS THIS UNDERSTANDING GROWS WITHIN YOU, USE THIS SPACE TO NOTE ANY MOMENTS WHERE YOU FEEL MORE CONNECTED TO NATURE, EVEN IN SMALL WAYS.

A SOFT LANDING

Let this spread be a place to settle into this new way of approaching plants. Bring in whatever stayed with you from the chapter, gently guiding your marks. You might feel like drawing how a plant feels, how it sees, or how it speaks to you.

First published in 2026 by OH
An Imprint of HEADLINE PUBLISHING GROUP LIMITED

1

Cataloguing in Publication Data is available from the British Library

ISBN 9781035435326

Printed and bound in China by C&C Offset Printing Co., Ltd.

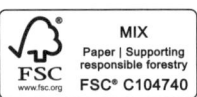

Headline's policy is to use papers that are natural, renewable and recyclable products and made from wood grown in well-managed forests and other controlled sources. The logging and manufacturing processes are expected to conform to the environmental regulations of the country of origin.

HEADLINE PUBLISHING GROUP LIMITED
An Hachette UK Company
Carmelite House
50 Victoria Embankment
London EC4Y 0DZ

The authorised representative in the EEA is Hachette Ireland,
8 Castlecourt Centre, Dublin 15, D15 XTP3, Ireland
(email: info@hbgi.ie)

www.headline.co.uk
www.hachette.co.uk